George Tremlett has been a rock writer almost since the music began in the mid-Fifties. He left King Edward VI School, Stratford-upon-Avon, in 1957 and then spent four years on *The Coventry Evening Telegraph* writing their daily TV column and reviewing all the visiting pop package shows.

In 1961 he moved to London and became a freelance writer, working part-time for *The New Musical Express*. He has since been London correspondent for TV and pop music magazines in Japan, Holland, Belgium, Germany, Australia, New Zealand, Finland, Sweden, and the United States. In this he is partnered by his wife, Jane. They also contribute to most major British teenage magazines.

Outside pop music journalism, George Tremlett pursues a political career as a member of the Greater London Council. For the past eleven years he has also been a councillor in Richmond-upon-Thames.

D1453363

Also by George Tremlett

THE DAVID BOWIE STORY
THE OSMOND STORY
THE GARY GLITTER STORY
THE DAVID ESSEX STORY

George Tremlett

The Rolling Stones Story

Futura Publications Limited

A Futura Book

First published in Great Britain in 1974
by Futura Publications Limited
Copyright © George Tremlett Limited 1974

ISBN 0 8600 7128 6
Printed in Great Britain by
C. Nicholls & Company Ltd.
The Philips Park Press
Manchester.

Futura Publications Limited
49 Poland Street,
LONDON W1A 2LG

ACKNOWLEDGEMENTS

It is a journalistic axiom that all good stories should answer the questions how, what, why, where and when. The success story of the Rolling Stones is so extraordinary in itself, so different from most rock music career biographies, that I have tried to fulfill that axiom. The 'what', the 'where' and the 'when' are answered in the first appendix which is the most detailed chronology so far published on the Stones' career, and is drawn from the files I have kept on the group since 1963. The 'how' is described in the book itself which draws on my own interviews with the Stones and those of the assistants I employed at the time, and particularly on interviews with different members of the Rolling Stones' families, notably Mick Jagger's brother, Chris, and also with Ian Stewart, who was originally a member of the group but who left it in 1963 and has been their road manager ever since, and also their recording manager, Jimmy Miller. As for the 'why'—well, read the book and draw your own conclusions.

CHAPTER ONE

Our story begins with one man—Alexis Korner. He was the catalyst that brought the Rolling Stones together, the man who inspired them, just as he did so many of the young rhythm 'n' blues fans who used to turn up in the audience at the club he ran in Ealing, West London. If one individual person deserves the title 'The Father of British Rock Music', then it is Korner, because he had an ear for talent, because he convinced so many young musicians that they had what it takes, and because he kept bringing so many of them into his band, or inviting them to join him on stage. Some have since become accomplished musicians even legendary figures—singers like Mick Jagger, Robert Plant, Eric Burdon, Paul Jones and Marsha Hunt; drummers like Charlie Watts and Ginger Baker; guitarists and keyboard musicians like Mick Taylor, Brian Jones, Keith Richard, Paul Williams, Hughie Flint, Colin Hodgkinson, Jack Bruce, Andy Fraser, Lee Jackson, Gerry Conway, Danny Thompson, Terry Cox and Graham Bond.

Besides the Stones, groups with ex-Korner musicians in their line-up have included Cream, Blind Faith, Airforce, Led Zeppelin, Back Door, Pentangle, The Nice, Manfred Mann, McGuinness Flint, Juicy Lucy, John Mayall's Bluesbreakers, Aynsley Dunbar's Retaliation, Nucleus and the Keef Hartley Band.

Most of them had one thing in common— they were all fans themselves back in 1961-3 when Korner was the main standard-bearer of rhythm 'n' blues in this country, leading his band Blues Incorporated with Alexis on guitar, the late Cyril Davies on harmonica, Charlie Watts on the drums, Jack Bruce on bass—a line-up that was quite variable since other musicians would step up on stage when invited. "It boils down to the fact that the first band in the field produces all the leaders," Charlie Watts once said in an interview with the now-defunct pop paper *Music Echo*. "When you consider Paul Jones used to come down from Oxford, Brian Jones from Cheltenham, and Eric Burdon from Newcastle—just to hear Blues Incorporated. And Mick, Brian, John Mayall, Graham Bond and Long John Baldry used to sit in on sessions . . . I left Blues Incorporated because I really wasn't good enough for Alexis' band. The others were such fantastic musicians, and I couldn't keep up the pace."

The keenest of them all at that time was Brian Jones, who used to travel regularly from Cheltenham to see Blues Incorporated, and then he would hang around the bar, excited to hear all the latest news and gossip, and the latest plans of the people he met each week at the club, before kipping down overnight on the floor at Korner's flat.

Jones, Jagger, Richard and most of the other young rhythm 'n' blues fans of the time were ex-Grammar School boys—some of whom had gone on to University, while others had dropped out of their middle class milieu, and taken well-paid jobs with no future; what they all had in common was this respect for Korner and the music he played.

Alexis was a man they could admire because he had always been true to himself—and had been a rebel for most of his life, too. He was born in Paris on April 19, 1928, of an Austrian father and a part Greek-part Turkish mother. His father was a cavalry officer in the Austrian army. In his early years, Alexis lived with various relatives here and on the Continent, being educated in France, Switzerland and North Africa as well as Britain. After leaving the cavalry his father had worked in numerous businesses—even drilling for oil in Abyssinia; but in the Thirties the family settled in London, and in 1938 his father took out British citizenship.

The young Alexis was asked to leave St. Paul's, the famous London public school—and even the Boy Scouts! And his parents decided to send him to a school for extremely disturbed children with high IQs. There, against his father's wishes, he turned to music, making his own guitar from plywood and a shaved-down table leg. After briefly working in the family shipping business, Alexis made music his career— working as an A & R man for Melodisc, as a publicist for Decca, and later with BBC Radio as a studio manager before finally becoming a musician himself in 1948 when he joined Chris Barber's jazz band, first playing piano, and then later, guitar. In the mid-Fifties, he played skiffle with Ken Colyer before briefly forming his own group and then working with Cyril Davies as a duo. They opened their own club in Soho, The Roundhouse Club, but that soon closed because very few people were interested in the music they were playing.

"Alexis and Cyril were undaunted," says the brief personal biography Alexis gave me the last time we spoke. "They simply became more determined than ever to make blues a valid form of music in Britain, so they invited visiting American bluesmen like Sonny Terry, Brownie McGee, Memphis Slim and Muddy Waters to sit in with them at the small clubs. Even the visiting Americans could not sway the English critics to like blues. In fact, Alexis and Cyril were becoming more popular in the USA than they were in Britain. Alexis was particularly influenced by Muddy Waters, an enthusiasm he was to share with Mick Jagger a few years later.

"Alexis and Cyril then decided to pioneer the blues further by playing on electric guitars, in a rhythm and blues style, which was louder and a less subtle form of music. At this stage, the laughter of the critics got even louder. Electric guitars for the blues were considered outrageous. The critics were not foreseeing what was about to happen in the Sixties, only a small band of musician fans in front of the bandstand named Mick Jagger, Keith Richard, Brian Jones, P. P. Pond (Paul Jones), and several others knew. They were getting Alexis' message, and he became "The Guv'nor" to this new generation of younger musicians who eventually made good under his aegis following Alexis' rebellious style. Alexis and Cyril decided to open up a R & B Club at a small pub in Ealing. They formed a band which Alexis called Blues Incorporated and on March 17th, 1962, the band began with Alexis on guitar, Cyril Davies blowing his harmonica, Dick Heckstall-Smith sporting his famous leather cap and playing tenor sax, and a slightly nervous drummer named Charlie Watts.

"A month or so later, Alexis was asked to take over Thursday night at the Marquee Club in Soho with

Blues Incorporated. Thursday had been a notoriously bad night for the Marquee, and on Alexis' opening night, 3rd May, 1962, there were only 127 people, but by the beginning of September they had developed a regular audience of 1,000 people in this small club. By the beginning of December, they were having to close the doors after half an hour. The Marquee management then decided it would be worthwhile for them to have Monday night so Alexis could even out the audience into a comfortable number. This didn't happen. Both nights became packed out and the R & B Boom was on its way. The Marquee became one of London's most popular clubs.

"Blues Incorporated at the Marquee were joined by a young Scotsman, Jack Bruce, lugging with him a bass of almost fungoid whiteness. In the new year of 1963, Charlie Watts left the band, and was replaced by another aspiring drummer named Ginger Baker. The band then moved over to the Flamingo and the lead singer was Mick Jagger . . . soon veterans of Blues Incorporated began to form other groups and a whole new wave of music evolved as The Rolling Stones and Manfred Mann hit the scene. John Mayall visited London and saw what Alexis was doing, and was so influenced he moved to London himself and formed his now famous Bluesbreakers in 1962."

Early that same year, Mick Jagger and Keith Richard met for the first time. It was during the rush hour at Dartford railway station on a platform packed with City men on their way to work and secretaries in spring dresses. Mick was waiting for a train to London where he was studying politics and economics at the London School of Economics (his mother expected him

11

to become a politician); Keith was en route to Sidcup School of Art, and under his arm—where everyone could see it—was a Chuck Berry album that he had had specially imported from Chess Studios in Chicago. The LP sleeve caught Jagger's attention, and they started talking, discovering that they had gone to the same primary school, that they shared the same friends —including guitarist Dick Taylor, who was also at Sidcup School of Art. They agreed to meet a few days later to hear each other's records and to see each other's guitars—and because his parents were expected to be more tolerant of the ensuing noise, this session was eventually held at Dick's house.

By then Brian Jones was busily trying to form a group of his own, and advertised for musicians in *Jazz News*—after all this time it is difficult to say who led who, who started what. But one thing is cerain; Brian Jones was then the driving force in what was to become the Rolling Stones—though before their line-up became formalised Mick had already started singing with Korner, and Brian was trying to persuade Paul Pond to give up his studies at Oxford University and be the Stones' singer (he failed, and Paul did not become a professional singer until Manfred Mann were formed some time later—by which time he was calling himself Paul Jones). Geoff Bradford was another early member of the Stones—and so was drummer Carlo Little and Keith's friend, Dick Taylor, and also pianist Ian Stewart, who is the Stones' road manager to this day.

"Mick didn't reply to that advertisement in *Jazz News*," Ian Stewart told me some time later. "He was now singing three nights a week with Korner and didn't have time for more. We spent weeks and months experimenting with different musicians and singers . . . and then later Mick left Korner to join us and he introduced us to Keith and Dick, and we had another re-shuffle to bring them in . . . it was very tricky trying to fit everything in because I still had a day-time job and so did Brian some of the time, and Mick was still at the LSE . . . and we still hadn't sorted out who was going to be drummer . . . Tony Chapman was with us for a while, and then Mick Avory who later joined The Kinks, and Carlo Little was with us, too, but the one drummer we were all keen on trying to persuade to come in with us was Charlie, whom we had all seen with Alexis, but that wasn't so easy to settle because we were still only rehearsing—and there was no money coming in."

The very first Rolling Stones' gig was at the Marquee —when they deputised for Alexis Korner and his Blues Incorporated, who had been offered their first radio broadcast that evening. Korner had wanted Jagger to join him on the programme, but seven years later he revealed in an interview with *The New Musical Express* that the plan had had to be abandoned— because he couldn't afford to pay Mick that night!

"As we were still quite a small name the BBC wouldn't pay for an extra singer, and as it happened Mick wasn't really bothered if he did the broadcast or not . . . so for that particular evening it was decided that Mick should team up with Keith Richard and Brian Jones, who together with Long John Baldry would 'dep' for us that evening at the Marquee. As it happened, this was to be the first gig by the Stones. And I missed the only opportunity of having Mick

13

record with the band! For unless someone taped us during our club appearances, there's no record of his stay with the band."

It was around this time that the other key figure in the early days of the Rolling Stones came into their lives, someone with a background as exotic as Alexis Korner's—and that was Giorgio Gomelski, son of a Russian doctor who had been born in the Caucasian mountains and had later practised in Moscow, and of a French mother. Before coming to London, Gomelski had hitch-hiked around the world, had organised the first Italian jazz festival, had lived in Chicago (which was how and where he became a passionate rhythm 'n' blues fan), and now he was running his own jazz club featuring the Dave Hunt Blues band—which had Ray Davies, later of the Kinks, as its guitarist.

"Sometimes the members of that band wouldn't turn up," Giorgio once told me. "Brian Jones, Mick Jagger and Keith Richard were in the club nearly every night —and they told me they were quite willing to perform for nothing. One night, Brian said to me: 'Look, Giorgio, you can't run a club without knowing whether your band's going to turn up! Give us a break. We'll do it for nothing.'

"So I gave them the break. And although they were good, the applause was hardly rapturous—because their music was so strange to the audience."

By now, Mick and Keith had moved into the small flat in Edith Grove, Fulham, that was now Brian Jones' home—and over in Richmond, Surrey, Mr. C. J. Buckle, landlord of the Station Hotel, was deciding to lease off his rear room, which was usually used for Masonic or Rotary functions, for occasional beat and jazz sessions. It was an old fashioned Victorian pub with a white-washed exterior badly needing a fresh coat of paint—and inside frosted glass partitions dividing the rooms, coal fires in the grates, and well-polished brass fittings. Johnny Dankworth leased the room for Monday night jazz sessions—and Giorgio Gomelski leased it for Sundays, calling it The Crawdaddy Club. The Rolling Stones appeared there every week; it was their first regular booking. Just before their residency began, Dick Taylor announced he was leaving. "I was fed up playing bass guitar—and in any case had to think about my exams," said Taylor, who was by then a student at the Royal College of Art, and later returned to music as a member of The Pretty Things. "There was no row or anything like that," he said. Bill Wyman took his place. And on the drums sat Charlie Watts. Their line-up was complete.

Gomelski saw them socially as well as on Sunday nights, and became their manager. "Mick, Brian and Keith were living in an appalling flat in Edith Grove," he told me. "It wouldn't have been so bad if they had cleaned it. I remember one night we went all over London sticking up posters with a big bucket of glue. When we had finished, rather than throw it away Mick and Keith asked me to give it to them. "We'll find some use for it,' said Mick.

"I went round to their flat about two weeks later and the abominable smell met me as they opened the door. Mick and Keith had filled up this glue bucket with cigarette ends, old toilet paper, old socks, anything. It was terrible.

"By then the Stones were doing very good business in Richmond and Brian Jones—the driving force behind them—kept pestering me to draw up a written contract. But I kept telling him that I could see no use in having a written contract if we couldn't trust one another."

CHAPTER TWO

In those early days, the Rolling Stone with the greatest determination to succeed was Brian Jones who then regarded it as his group. After all, it was he who placed that advertisement in *Jazz News*—and he was the one who wanted to form a new group while Mick, Keith and Charlie were all still happily working with Alexis Korner. And he was also the one who made the greatest effort to see Korner live, travelling up from Cheltenham nearly every week until he found a flat of his own—and became the first member of the menage to acquire total independence.

As well as being determined, Jones was also enigmatic even to his closet friends; they could not understand him—even though it was generally agreed that he possessed personal charm, was good company socially, was fascinating to women, and could converse on almost any subject.

Jones was fun—but he also brought more misery and unhappiness to those unfortunate enough to be involved with him than probably any other musician who has ever worked in the British music business. In retrospect, his life seems to have been a sordid waste which is sad because he had so much else to offer.

My own feeling, having met him occasionally and having known many people who worked with him and who knew him intimately, is that he was probably in need of prolonged mental treatment long before he joined the Rolling Stones. While he was still alive,

Giorgio Gomelski told me that he thought Brian was very sick and "a boy who should have had treatment; his responses were never those of a normal person".

Even now, I am not going to reveal all I know about him since this would be distasteful and now that he is dead it is better not to distress those who remember him with affection (as many do), but it should be said that few people deserve less to be posthumous folk heroes than Lewis Brian Hopkin-Jones, a man who rarely did a noble deed, who had at least six illegitimate children by different women, who neglected to maintain his children, who often treated their mothers shamefully, who had countless other sexual relationships (often several at a time), who was an habitual liar, and frequently introduced his friends to drugs.

And yet, back in the early Sixties, Jones was a man with the world at his feet. He was, as the Lord Chief Justice (Lord Parker) himself said some years later when Jones appealed against one of his drug convictions, "a very intelligent young man". He was born in Cheltenham on February 28th, probably in 1942 (his age and height were two subjects he frequently lied about), the first child of Mr. and Mrs. Lewis Hopkin-Jones. Brian's sister Barbara was born four years later. Their father had been to university, gained a Bachelor of Science degree, and worked as an engineer in the aircraft industry. He was an organist in the local church and had been secretary of the choral society.

At school, Brian was an outstanding pupil, expected to go to university himself, possibly to begin training as a dentist. He won a place at the Cheltenham Grammar School and in his General Certificate of Examination gained the exceptional results of nine passes at Ordinary-level and two at Advanced-level. But, to the distress of his family, Jones spurned the opportunities that were offered to him, and began to drift from one dead-end job to another. He worked behind the counter in a record shop that went bankrupt, worked for an optician, then in the sports department of a store and in a factory at Brockworth near Cheltenham (he injured his leg and lost a tooth being driven to work one morning by another worker at the factory, when the van overturned).

His first illegitimate child was by a fourteen year old schoolgirl, who gave the baby away for adoption at birth; his second was by a sixteen year old girl whom he met in a local coffee bar. While both were pregnant, his affairs continued with other girls—and he also drifted from job to job, working briefly as a coalman and then as a bus conductor, before eventually getting a job in February, 1961, as a trainee in the architectural department of Gloucestershire County Council. He divided his spare time between playing with a local group, the Ramrods, and day-dreaming in the Aztec coffee bar, where he kept telling his friends that what he most wanted to do was to go to London, play with a band and become a star.

Years later in an interview with *Disc Weekly*, Jones said: "I suppose you could call me a bit of a rebel. My father wanted me to go to university. But I didn't fancy that. And I didn't like the idea of working for anyone who could boss me around." He told the *New Musical Express*: "I started drifting and got interested in drinks, girls and things, so I jacked it all in and did exactly as I pleased. What has proved to be the ruination of many people has been the making of me. I went against everything I had been brought up to believe in." He even claimed that he had spent a whole year hitch-hiking around the Continent.

After falling out with his parents, he moved into a flat in Parabola Road, Cheltenham, and then to another in Pitfield Square, going regularly to a jazz club in Bishops Cleeve when his own band did not have an engagement. Now happy in his work, he was hoping to gain a scholarship at the local art college. He was offered a place—but the offer was withdrawn. "Apparently someone had written to the college to say that Brian was irresponsible and a drifter," said the mother of his second child, Pat Andrews.

Music was now becoming the main interest in his life. He had started to play guitar soon after leaving school. "At first I think it was only a hobby," said his mother Mrs. Louisa Jones. "He had always been keen on music and started piano lessons when he was six or seven. When he was twelve, Brian joined the school orchestra and learned clarinet, but I don't think he has played that much since . . . he was very keen on sports at school, particularly cricket, table tennis and judo, and one thing he really excelled at was diving, although he wasn't particularly interested in swimming itself."

Now these past pursuits were forgotten, but like so many other young musicians living far from London Brian had no idea how to set about moving to the big city and gaining contacts there. His 'break', for that was what it turned out to be, came in 1961 when Alexis Korner played a gig in Cheltenham with Chris Barber, and afterwards got talking to Brian in the Wine Patio which was just across the road from the jazz club. Conversationally, Brian had a maturity beyond his years, and Korner was immediately impressed by his enthusiasm and his knowledge of rhythm and blues.

They started talking about guitars and different musicians, and Brian mentioned how difficult it was to know what step to take next. Korner offered to try to find work for him, and said that he could stay at his flat while looking for somewhere to live. After that, Brian kept in touch with Korner by phone, and started travelling regularly up to London to see Blues Incorporated play at the club in Ealing. Eventually he dropped everything in Cheltenham to move into a flat in Weech Road, West Hampstead, with the mother of his second child, Pat Andrews. Later they had flats in Powis Square, Notting Hill Gate, and in Edith Grove, Fulham. Brian worked first in the sports department at Whiteleys, the Queensway department store, and then at the Civil Service Stores in the Strand, while Pat took a job in a laundry. Between them they earned £16-17 a week, spending most of it on records and trips to different jazz clubs.

At the club in Ealing, Alexis Korner introduced Brian to his drummer, Charlie, to Mick Jagger, who sang with Blues Incorporated occasionally, and to Keith Richard, who sometimes sat in on guitar. They met regularly after that, and it wasn't long before they were talking of forming a group together. This they did, calling themselves The Rollin' Stones (with the apostrophe), and rehearsing over a pub in Soho. Bill Wyman came in through an advertisement in a music paper, and Charlie Watts joined some months later.

As the group became successful, Brian Jones reacted

to the pressures that resulted in a different way to the others. "Brian was determined to be a star at any price," Gomelski once told me. "When they were appearing at Richmond, Brian was the driving force behind them—and he kept pestering me to draw up a written contract, but I didn't believe in that. I remember when the Beatles were appearing at the Albert Hall, Brian was mistaken for a Beatle as he walked in the stage door, and was mobbed. He loved it, and told me afterwards: 'Giorgio—it was a lovely feeling. That's how I want it to be.' Of course, the Beatles had been to watch the Stones at Richmond and thought the group was wonderful. Many times John and Paul came back to my flat for soup and omelettes, talking with the Stones about music into the early hours. Then we moved the club to larger premises, and I decided to make a film of our first concert. I had only just finished that when my father died and I had to look after the funeral arrangements. When I came back to England, the film was ready for showing and we all sat down together in the flat to see it. The last person to arrive was Brian Jones, who had with him a strange young man called Loog. I asked who he was, and Brian told me he was an old school friend from Cheltenham . . . the next thing I knew was that the Stones had signed a written contract with this chap Loog, and I discovered that his real name was Andrew Loog Oldham . . . I thought we had a verbal understanding, and I felt tremendously let down when they left me. I was very upset by it."

As their records became steadily more successful, selling in greater numbers and encouraging promoters to book them for tours, Brian Jones seemed to take it all in his stride, changing his life-style as his income increased, moving to well-furnished flats in Chelsea, and thus into a different social world. Of all the Stones at that time, he seemed to have the widest circle of friends, being adventurous in his choice of food, and going out with friends most nights of the week—evenings that usually ended with parties at his latest Chelsea home. John Lennon, Paul McCartney, Gordon Waller, Joey Paige—these were among the friends who were in and out of his home, and he in theirs, night after night.

His friendships were deep and genuine—he was a generous host, had no religious or racial prejudices (he hated colour prejudice), would help anyone if he could, would talk for hours on end about politics and social problems, and whereas many other people in the music business looked scruffy day and night, Brian seldom did—he had a range of three-piece suits in his wardrobe, a selection of well cut shirts and silk ties, and had a social grace that many of his contemporaries noticeably lacked.

But underneath it all, he was deeply mixed-up, very insecure, acutely conscious about his height, jealous of whoever was the girl of the moment—and forever getting madly enthusiastic about different ideas that seldom held their attraction for long. One of his secret passions was buses—he had an almost encyclopedic knowledge about which Corporation acquired which bus when, where they ran, how many miles they travelled to the gallon, what their numbers were, where they were made, what their defects were (it was something he seldom talked about because he hated people laughing at him—and thought this would make him a joke). Once he started handling large sums of money, Brian even started buying buses that caught his fancy. I can well remember the consternation one day when I was in his manager's office and someone who had sold Brain a double decker bus phoned up asking where it should be delivered. No-one knew what to say because he lived in a tiny flat in Chelsea without a garage!

This bizarrely impractical attitude of mind revealed itself in other ways. He was forever planning new companies, new businesses and new groups—sparking off constant rumours within the music business that he would leave the Stones. If the group visited Paris, then for a few days Paris would be his sole topic of conversation and he would tell all his friends he was going to live there—but the following week it could be Amsterdam, Munich, New York or Brussels! And he took it all so very seriously. Brian Jones could never take a joke against himself.

CHAPTER THREE

When the Rolling Stones started, there was one other person with a driving ambition—and that was Mick Jagger. He was their singer and apart from harmonica, played no other instrument on stage. But that did not matter; his mere presence on stage with pouting lips and mincing dance contributed more to the group than any other single factor. So far as their fans and the press were concerned, he became *The* Stone, with every misadventure chronicled in the morning papers. Jagger had one trait unusual in artistes (though not now); he read carefully every contract the Rolling Stones signed—though they were to live to regret signing some of them.

Although his image was that of the rebel, the leader of youth, Jagger came from a secure and conventional middle class background—his family home was a spacious, white-pebbled detached house, surrounded by trees, in Wilmington, on the outskirts of Dartford, Kent, where he and his younger brother Chris were brought up by their parents, Joe and Eva Jagger. His father was a physical training instructor and University lecturer, and encouraged his son to be studious. Mick was only seventeen years old when he won a scholarship from Dartford Grammar School to the London School of Economics.

"I always had the feeling that Mike would be something," said his mother. "He was a very adventurous boy when he was younger, but then later he became interested in money. It always struck us as odd. Money doesn't usually interest little boys, but it did Mike. He didn't want to be a pilot or an engine driver—he wanted a lot of money! He suddenly realised that though he could still become a lawyer or a politician, which was what I thought he would be, the rewards would come so late in life that he'd be too old to enjoy them. Mick suddenly wanted to join the 'get rich quick' stakes. He told me he was throwing up his University course. For months on end, I seemed to lose touch with him."

As with Brian Jones' parents, Mr. and Mrs. Jagger could be forgiven and understood if they ever thought that Mick was throwing away all his chances; like Brian, he could have gained a good University degree. But, though he would regularly work past midnight on an essay that caught his imagination or a book that seemed relevant, Mick was none too keen on the thought of spending years as a student. His brother Chris once told me what he remembered of Mick at the time.

"Mick wasn't madly fond of school," he said. "His pet hates were compulsory games, bad school dinners and school uniform. Regularly—once or twice a week —he would get caught without his school cap, and would have to do some lines as a punishment. And those dinners! They were a joke with the boys. When the cook left after about thirty years, Mick and his friends thought she still had a lot to learn—so they presented her with a cookery book!

"He was really pretty good at games, though not rough ones like Rugby football. Basketball and Bad-minton were more in Mick's line. He also liked cricket,

26

and played for the First XI on several occasions—but only on weekdays if he could help it. Mick didn't like school sport interfering with his weekends. Even then, he was mad on music. He was about fifteen when the skiffle craze started in England, and formed a couple of groups of his own. We still have one of Mick's exercise books at home in which he wrote an essay on how to form a skiffle group. 'Before any group is started up,' he wrote, 'there should be someone who can sing really well and a couple of guitarists who can play good strong chords.'

"He bought his first guitar when we were all on holiday in Spain, but it wasn't a very good guitar and now lies, a bit battered, in a corner of my bedroom with one string and Mick's old pyjama cord around its neck. Still, he got a fairly good sound out of it. It was only when Keith and Dick Taylor came round practising that Mick thought more about playing the harmonica and singing—actually he was never called Mick then. We all called him Mike. He hated the name Mick, and I only used it when I was teasing him. But after he left school, the name sort of stuck."

When the Rolling Stones started recording, Mick became something of a local hero at his old school, Dartford Grammar. At the Founders' Day celebrations when all the famous past pupils' names were read out, there were cries of 'What about Mick Jagger, then?' from the back of the hall. All his signatures were cut from his old text books—and one boy even sawed off the chunk from Mick's old desk where he had carved his name.

"When Mick was still at home, he used to take vacation jobs to earn some extra cash," said Chris

Jagger. "Once he even worked as a porter in the local mental hospital . . . while he was still at the LSE, Mick left home and moved into the flat in Edith Grove with Brian and Keith. That was a real hole—but a homely sort of hole. They used to put me up there sometimes. It was a scruffy little flat, just two rooms. The main piece of furniture was a record player, and in the middle of the main room a bare electric light bulb was their only lighting."

Another person who visited Mick and the others there regularly was Ian Stewart, originally the sixth member of the Rollin' Stones, playing the piano. He used to drive them all to their gigs in a Volkswagen van that he had bought by selling all the shares he had been given as an employee of ICI under a scheme to encourage staff to become share-owners in the company. "Every night I used to pick them up, and at that time they were starving . . . Bill and I were buying them food with what little money was left over from our own wages. I used to call there straight from work, about 5 or 6 p.m., and they would all still be in bed. They lived there through a freezing cold winter, and as they had no money for the electric meter or for food, they just stayed in bed all day to keep warm.

"They were always getting up to jokes. One of the crudest was their lavatory. Anyone who went there thought the wires entwined around the cistern were all part of the Stones' peculiar amplifying system, but the wires actually connected a microphone in the lavatory to a tape recorder in another room, whch was duly played back to the acute embarrassment of anyone who called at the flat."

Another joke was played on Brian Jones, then working in a record shop. One day a woman part-exchanged her old gramophone for a new model, and Brian was given the old one. He was delighted with it, carried it back to Edith Grove—and then one night when he switched it on there was a flash of flame and a cloud of smoke. Keith had plugged his earth into the light socket! "For months Mick and Keith were in stitches every time Brian talked about getting his record player mended, but he never knew what they were laughing about," said Stewart. "Then another time when we were on tour, Brian's bed was made into an apple pie—and he didn't like that, either!"

The only person who foresaw their later success while the three of them lived in Edith Grove was a woman called Judith Credland, a fully-trained pharmacist, who had the flat beneath them. The Stones were then penniless. "If there was ever any food in the flat at all, it was just a few buns and a packet of margarine —and that was when they were well off," said Ian Stewart. "They lived on coffee and their biggest crisis would be to finish a jar.

"Judy would always help them out. They would creep down to her kitchen at 3 or 4 a.m. in the morning for the odd jar, and leave scribbled IOUs on the draining board for when she woke up. Judy was marvellous and she would do anything to help the boys. She frequently used to come up to sit with us in the evenings, making coffee and listening to records. Her great hobby was palm reading, and one night she read our hands one by one.

"She took Mick's hand in hers, and as he opened his fingers she gasped: 'You've got the Star of Fame. It's all there!' Keith and Brian laughed. None of us took that seriously then. But Mick has often talked about it since, and Judy is still a good friend of ours. She now lives in Los Angeles and we see her every time we go over there."

What kind of person was Mick Jagger at that time in his career? How had he changed since childhood? Different people who knew him, within his family and outside, formed varying impressions. "He is a very emotional person, and if you upset him it goes deep," Ian Stewart once told me. "An incident like that palm-reading session will make a lasting impression on Mick. He has that kind of temperament, but at the same time he is an excellent businessman. He vets every deal, and examines all the Stones' contracts before they are signed."

In an interview with the now-defunct magazine *Today*, Mick's mother, Mrs. Eva Jagger, said he was "no more of a rebel than any other boy of his age", and remembered that the first sign he showed of being interested in music was when he used to sing himself to sleep as a child. Later, he loved military bands and his grandmother used to take him regularly to hear the local Salvation Army band. "Mick was never very demonstrative," said Mrs. Jagger. "He didn't show his feelings much, but I know he loves his family. And he was always thoughtful. If ever he decided to stay overnight at a friend's house, he would never fail to telephone and let me know." On another occasion, Mrs. Jagger recalled: "We went through a Tarzan period when the boys would swing from branch to branch giving out loud cries and screams. They used to terrify me sometimes, sitting for what seemed like hours high up some tree. I was always afraid they would fall . . . Mick was a good boy most of the time, except for one period when he was about four years old. I remember once when we were on holiday, walking along a beach one day, and Mick knocked down every single sandcastle we came across, even ones that little boys were still building.

"He was always interested in pop music and used to play records for hours. After leaving a song on the record player only a couple of times, he knew the words and could sing them," continued Mrs. Jagger. "But I don't think Mick considered making music his career until he started practising with Keith Richard and Dick Taylor . . . and I must admit that when he first started out with the Rolling Stones, I was very worried. There seemed no future to it all, and it was taking up all his time."

Chrissie Shrimpton, sister of famous model Jean Shrimpton and one of Mick's earliest girlfriends (for a long while in the early Sixties they were inseparable and were expected to marry) saw another side of Jagger. At the time she told me: "He's the sort of boy I want to mother. The very first time I saw him—on a TV programme with the Stones—I thought he looked thin, ill and pathetic, and I thought he really needed someone to give him a jolt. We were introduced at a party a few weeks later, and fell for each other immediately . . . there were times when I wanted to scream. Mick often wouldn't eat for days—not because he couldn't afford it, but because he just hadn't got his life organised. He'd turn up for dates at least two hours late, and then say very little—just sit and sort of stare with a little smile on his lips. It took me about three months to discover that Mick wasn't really weird or in need of a psychiatrist. He was just wrapped up in the Stones. If Brian Jones had a problem, they all shared it. They are not individuals in this respect— what happens to one—happens to all of them.

"Mick would call at my flat to take me out to the pictures and stand in the doorway, smiling shyly and looking for all the world like a little boy lost. Often, I'd ask him if he'd eaten and he would airily reel off a list of meals that he'd had in the past twenty-four hours. But I soon learned how to catch him out. He's the sort of person who can't lie. When this happened, I'd tell him off, fling on my apron and start to cook. I can't tell you how many times our dates have been spent in the kitchen. I know I have changed Mick's way of dressing. When I first knew him, he'd wear anything provided it wasn't smart—going for the most ludicrous way-out clothes, and then wearing them until they nearly dropped off his back. When we started shopping together, I'd encourage him to spend as much as he could on clothes. If there was a shirt he liked, I'd persuade him to buy two or three—not just one. Gradually, I saw him change. Now he wears smart sports jackets and well-pressed, tapered slacks. He's getting a nice collection of ties, too.'

As the Stones' career developed through 1963-5, Mick's life broadened, though his parents noticed that his old interest in politics seemed to be diminishing. In his spare time, he would drive out to Buckinghamshire to go horse-riding with Chrissie Shrimpton at her parents' farm; sometimes he would vanish for a few days to the Continent to visit art galleries and museums; he became keen on tennis, following the Wimbledon games avidly on TV; visiting Australia and the States with the Stones, he turned to water-skiing as another relaxation.

If it is true that you can tell a man by his friends, then here, too, there were signs that his personality was widening. In the evenings he would regularly be seen dining at Chelsea restaurants like the Casserole, and then visiting the then popular Ad Lib and Cromwellian clubs. "Other evenings, he will just stay at home and listen to records," said Chris Jagger. "When he came back from his last American trip, he was raving about a jazz organist called John Patten. He is also very keen on Charlie Mingus, and has a large collection of spiritual and gospel LPs. One of the few groups he really raves about is The Who." For a time, Mick lived at the home of David Bailey, the photographer, who became one of his closet friends.

Other close friends were The Beatles, especially Lennon with whom Jagger seemed to feel a special affinity. "They got on so well together because they are both good conversationalists," said Chris Jagger. "John went to art college and at one time wanted to become a journalist; Mick had been to University and shared an interest in art and music . . . there was one night when John stayed all night at Mick's flat listening to records he had brought back from the States. John left around 6 a.m. in the morning, just as the milkmen were starting their rounds, and couldn't find a taxi anywhere—so he caught an Underground train home instead, travelling through London with a crowd of office cleaners on their way to work, and none of them recognised him."

CHAPTER FOUR

The two closest friends within the Rolling Stones when they started were Mick Jagger and Keith Richard. It is a relationship with deep roots. They were both brought up in the same area, Dartford in Kent, and although they did not become close friends until their late teens both had been to the same primary school as children.

Keith was an only child, and the family name is really Richards—he dropped the final "s" when choosing a stage name at the beginning of his career as a musician (the only Stone who completely changed his name was Bill Wyman, whose real name is Perks). Keith's mother, Mrs. Doris Richards, used to work selling washing machines as a demonstrator in the Co-op store in Dartford. He has always been very close to her.

"Keith was always a bit of a mother's boy as a child," Mrs. Richards once said. "When he started school, he used to get panic-stricken if I wasn't there waiting for him when he and all the other kids came out of school. I think he got fairly spoilt because he was the first boy in the family. I had come from a family of seven girls, which meant that he had six aunts, who all had a soft spot for him because he really was a sweet-looking kid. He always looked so chubby and sturdy, with a nose that always seemed to be shining red."

As a child, Keith was always generous towards his mother—a trait that has continued since he became a

Rolling Stone. His gifts to his mother have ranged from a new Austin 1100 car to items of jewellery such as an antique fob watch and a gold cigarette lighter. "He was always like that as a child, constantly saving up his pennies to buy birthday or Christmas presents, or to get me a box of chocolates. He would always far rather spend money on other people than on himself, and he was the sort of person who would never forget people's birthdays . . . yet the funny thing was that he was also a loner, and seemed to prefer his own company to being in a group. He joined the Boy Scouts at one stage, but left after a few weeks—and he didn't like playing Rugby football at all. When his form went out cross country running, Keith would always get out of it when he could, slipping behind a tree to hide . . . he was always fond of animals, and I can remember him once bringing home a white mouse because he said he was afraid that the boy who owned it was going to kill it. We kept it in a cage and Keith looked after it very carefully until one day, while we were all out, the mouse escaped and we never saw it again. He was heart-broken over that . . . as he grew up, Keith became very independent. Having always done so much for him, I was afraid that he would be hopelessly lost when he left home. But it didn't turn out like that at all."

Keith's interest in music started in his early teens, and when he was 15 his mother bought him a guitar for £10. From that day, it has been the most important thing in his life," she said. "My father used to run a dance band before the war, and he taught Keith a few chords—but the rest he has taught himself. One of his great ambitions is to be able to play really well."

Until that meeting on the platform at Dartford railway station, Keith's ambitions had been artistic rather than musical; he had progressed from Dartford Technical School to Sidcup School of Art, where he spent three years training himself for a career in advertising. (Although it's a side of him that is rarely seen, Keith is to this day a skilled cartoonist.) Before going to the college, Keith had been a semi-Teddy Boy, proud of his pink socks and drainpipe trousers. But art college changed all that; he became much more Bohemian, and his interest in music was encouraged by a friendship with Dick Taylor, who later left the Stones himself just before Charlie joined to take up a course at the Royal College of Art.

"Dick was always trying to persuade Keith to join a group," said Mrs. Richards. "But although he was so keen on playing the guitar, for some reason he wouldn't until he met Mick, and then he changed his mind. From then on, the three of them spent every possible hour practising together at their different homes."

By the time he finished his three year course, Keith's mind was made up; instead of going into advertising he moved into the Edith Grove flat with Brian and Mick—and then later when the Stones were signed to a management contract by Andrew Loog Oldham and Eric Easton, he and Mick moved on to another much more comfortable flat in Mapesbury Road, Hampstead, North London.

It was here that he and Mick started to write songs together; a partnership that was to bring the Rolling Stones their most successful records—and because of the songwriting royalties was to make Mick and Keith by far the wealthiest members of the group (it's often

36

forgotten that the Stone's earliest hits were mainly cover versions of songs/hits by other artistes—*Come On* was a Chuck Berry number; *I Wanna Be Your Man* was written for them by John Lennon and Paul McCartney; *Not Fade Away* was an old Buddy Holly number; *Little Red Rooster* was written by Willie Dixon and had been a hit for Sam Cooke).

The flat was always comfortably untidy with ashtrays full of scraps of paper, orange peel and old cigarette ends; with newspapers and magazines scattered around the floor (Mick has always been a voracious reader), and LPs by the rhythm 'n' blues artistes they both so admired, Chuck Berry, John Lee Hooker, Muddy Waters, etc. They divided their main room into two; one part a lounge and the other a dining room, with a modern, light wood table and matching chairs, while at the other end of the room there were old, well-worn armchairs and a sofa.

"This is how we like the place to be," said Keith at the time. "We spend most of our time here when we aren't touring, rarely going out . . . most nights we just concentrate on writing new songs, often staying up until four or five in the morning. Mind you, we don't get up until mid-day—and some days not until tea-time."

Soon, Mick and Keith started writing songs for other artistes, too—*As Tears Go By* for Marianne Faithful; *Blue Turns To Grey* for Cliff Richard; *That Girl Belongs To Yesterday* for Gene Pitney; *Sittin' On A Fence* for Twice As Much; *Out Of Time* for Chris Farlowe, as well as all the Stones' own hits after *The Last Time*. Soon they had five different companies handling their copyrights—companies with such strange names as Nanker and Phelge Music Ltd. and Porthdyke Ltd.

"We kept coming up with names that the Registrar of Companies had already registered, so we let him find one in the end—I think he just had Porthdyke floating about free," said Keith. Some time after this I interviewed Mick and Keith together on their song-writing, and Jagger told me: "I suppose people are never going to believe it, but we just don't know how much money we are making . . . all our money is looked after by an accountant. At the end of the year, a lump sum is paid into our personal account—a sum that has accumulated from record royalties, personal appear-ances, Performing Rights, merchandising, and so on . . . we've no idea which individual song or personal appearance it comes from. I once asked to see some specific figures and the accountant gave me a list of things which was just a jumble of figures to me."

Keith commented: "After one thousand pounds comes ten thousand pounds—and then after that it means nothing. It's just a lot of money. You don't think about it . . . I suppose our most successful com-position in terms of royalties must have been *Satisfac-tion* which has now been recorded by over sixty dif-ferent artistes all over the world, but we've no idea how much it has earned. It's still earning—I hope. That is probably the only number which we feel has been better interpreted by another artist—we preferred Otis Red-ding's version to our own . . . Mick usually writes the lyrics and I write the music. You just get an idea—a phrase like I can't get no satisfaction or Get off of my cloud and you build from it. One idea leads to another."

"I generally sit down and just write continuously

until I come to the end of a progression of ideas. I seldom come back to something. It's a strange thing, but I always get the biggest kick out of the anticipation of a song. It's the knowledge of having written something which might be our next single which is the real kick. By the time it's out on the market I've forgotten it and we're generally writing the next one," said Keith.

"The songs we're writing cannot be compared with those by Cole Porter, Irving Berlin or Rodgers and Hammerstein," said Jagger. "They were written for the sophisticated. Their songs are now called standards —they're old songs, that's all. Written for people of 25-30 about an age that has mostly passed. You play something long enough and often enough and everyone says it's a standard—*Long Tall Sally* must be a standard now."

This prompted Keith to say: 'When someone in a tuxedo with greasy hair like Frank Sinatra comes along and records one of our songs then maybe we'll have a standard, too . . . the Irving Berlin type of music was founded on a basis of light opera and jazz. Our music is drawn from the influences of white and negro folk music. We try to reflect forward-looking attitudes. You have to be progressive when you write for young people."

"Progression in music can even go backwards. Look at the Troggs. They are experimenting with simplicity —it's a form of progression. Dylan is a progressive writer. You only have to listen to *Blonde On Blonde* and then his early albums to see how far he has gone. People just aren't sympathetic to Bob Dylan. They said that *Rainy Day Woman* was rubbish, but if you'd been stoned and listened to the disc you would have understood," said Keith, smiling as Mick went on to stress the importance of being ahead of one's audience.

"This is where people like Billy Graham fall down," he said. "He is dealing with and talking of a morality which is no longer related to young people. His teachings are based upon illustrations from times that are no longer today. Tomorrow's people can never be communicated with by yesterday's voice."

CHAPTER FIVE

Possibly the happiest, the most fulfilled and certainly the most enimatic member of the Rolling Stones is their drummer Charlie Watts, and he has seemed like that ever since he became the last one to join the group in January, 1963. Because he seldom spoke in interviews, Charlie was dubbed "The Silent Stone". Because he often smiled and still said little, his expression was compared to that of the Mona Lisa. Once when interviewed by *The Melody Maker*, Charlie said: "I give the impression of being bored, but I'm not really. I've just got an incredibly boring face." Right from the start he had a maturity and a quiet contentment, and I have often suspected myself, that despite the publicity Jagger receives, and the fact that he has been treated by the press as though he were the spokesman for his generation, Charlie Watts probably has the best-developed intellect of all the Rolling Stones.

The trouble with Charlie is that he rarely does himself justice. He is polite, modest and rarely allows anyone outside the group to scratch much below the surface. He manages to protect his privacy better than the other members of the group, and like Bill Wyman he was never involved in any of the drug scandals that dogged Jagger, Richard and Jones through the late sixties; he and Bill both have a reputation within the music business for being totally "straight". The truth quite simply was that while success went to Brian Jones' head and eventually helped to destroy him, and

41

while drugs of different kinds became accepted within the menage that included Jagger and Richard, Charlie Watts always had had and adhered to a much more conventional life.

He was born in June, 1941, and brought up in a prefab in Neasden, going on from the Tylers Croft school, where he won several prizes for Art and English, to the Harrow College of Art. "Charlie was a big boy with strong legs, and he loved games, especially football, and was forever coming home with dirty knees and muddy clothes," said his mother. "We often thought he would become a footballer; even now he would cross a road to kick a stone. His father was even more proud when he won those prizes at school than he is about the Stones' success. We wanted Charlie to go in for graphic art or draughtsmanship, and were very pleased when he went on to Harrow . . . Charlie always wanted a drum kit, and used to rap out tunes on the table with pieces of wood or a knife and fork. We bought him his first set of drums for Christmas when he was fourteen. It cost £12. He took to it straight away, and often used to sit at home playing jazz records and accompanying them on his drum set. The neighbours were very good; they never complained."

After leaving the art college, Charlie worked as draughtsman and designer with the Charles Hobson and Gray advertising agency, in the evenings he started earning extra money as a drummer, eventually joining Alexis Korner's Blues Incorporated, and it was because of his work in that band that he was later offered a place in the Rolling Stones.

"I met Alexis in a club somewhere," said Charlie

in an interview with *The New Musical Express* in 1964, "and he asked me if I'd play drums for him. A friend of mine, Andy Webb, said I should join the band, but I had to go to Denmark to work in design so I sort of lost touch with things . . . while I was away, Alexis formed his band, and I came back to England with Andy. I joined the band with Cyril Davies, and Andy used to sing with us . . . we had some great guys in the band like Jack Bruce."

It was through this band that he met Brian, Mick and Keith. In that same interview, Charlie continued: "We were playing at a club in Ealing, and they used to come along and sometimes sit in. It was a lot different then. People used to come up to the stand and have a go, and the whole thing was great . . . we were doing so much work that I couldn't keep up with what Alexis wanted. It was a very different scene—Alexis Korner was very big . . . the Rolling Stones were the only band I met who were playing without being paid. It was great, though—so I joined them. Then, after a while, we started getting paid. It was marvellous, you know, getting paid for doing something like that."

For the first few months after he joined the group, Charlie continued to work at the advertising agency, amusing the others by the way he turned up at the flat at Edith Grove sometimes with an easel under his arm to ask if there was a gig that night. Even then he looked different to the other Stones—nearly always in a suit with shirt collar and tie, and much shorter hair than theirs. He even had a collection of over a hundred pocket handkerchiefs which caused the others to nickname him Beau Brummell! Then and until he married, Charlie lived at home with his parents, who were worried when he eventually gave up the advertising job to become a full-time Rolling Stone.

"Charlie had always taken pride in his appearance, something he took from his Dad," said Mrs. Watts. "His Dad used to go with him to buy all his clothes until he was seventeen, and until he met the Stones Charlie always had short hair . . . his sister Linda used to cut it for him. Charlie would never trust a barber. I was worried when he gave up his job. He was still living at home and we had to keep him. Of course, I hoped the group would do well—but I never imagined they would be as big as they did become . . . Charlie does sometimes give people this impression that he is moody, but he isn't really being nasty. It's just that he gets very involved in his own thoughts. Charlie is very warm-natured, in fact."

As the Rolling Stones became successful, Charlie seemed to take it all in his stride much more easily than the others—marrying Shirley in 1964 (without telling the others), first setting up home in a flat in Paddington, then buying a house in Lewes, Sussex, before buying his present home, a Sussex country estate that had formerly been the home of Lord Shawcross, and which had in the 16th century, been a hunting lodge for the first Archbishop of Canterbury.

As well as his ever-growing collection of modern jazz albums that he had first started to assemble in his teens, Charlie and Shirley now started to collect antique furniture, souvenirs of the American Civil War, a collection of Victorian dolls (Shirley's hobby), rare and antiquarian books, ornaments and paintings. They equipped one room as a studio for Shirley to continue her work as a sculptor; Charlie had another where he could work on his own projects—most have remained private and unpublished, but he did write and illustrate a book on the American jazzman Charlie Parker, *Ode To A High Flying Bird*, and also illustrated two children's books. And although his talents seemed to flourish, Charlie was always too modest to talk about them; his sense of privacy was always there.

In October, 1964, he had suddenly married Shirley, whom he had then known for three years since they first met when he was playing with Alexis Korner at a London club. Their marriage was in secret at a register office in Bradford, Yorkshire, on October 14th, and news of it did not leak out until five weeks later when Charlie told *The Daily Mail*: "Yes, I am married. I kept it a secret from the boys. I thought that if the news leaked out, it would have a bad effect on them. I intended keeping it a secret as long as I could. When I told my mates—I had to—their reaction was just, 'Oh, that's nice. You got married'."

After revealing how he and Shirley had first met, Charlie said: "She was one of the audience when I spotted her. I liked her and asked her for a date. We've been courting ever since, except for a short break. I proposed six months ago and she accepted. That's it, I suppose. Now everyone will know. I tried to keep it a secret. I wanted it to be a secret. But I suppose if Kruschev can't keep a secret, neither can I."

Shirley told the paper: "We have wanted to marry for about a year and just didn't dare. We thought it would harm Charlie's career. But the months went on and we decided we could not live separately any longer ... we decided on the secret wedding at Bradford only a few days beforehand. It was all such a terrible rush.

45

We had to get a three-day special licence and we knew that if Charlie was given a last-minute recording job all our plans would be ruined. I don't remember much about the actual ceremony, it was all so quick. We slipped into the side door to get married without anyone seeing."

The Registrar, Mr. J. R. Hinkins, was pledged to secrecy—and didn't even tell his own daughter. And one of the two witnesses, Mr. Andy Hoogenboom, a friend of Charlie's, said: "Charlie and Shirley were so much in love they just wanted to get married as soon as possible. The only way out seemed to be to tell no-one, not even his manager or the group."

Charlie has been just as secretive ever since, developing a life-style quite different to most of his contemporaries in the music business; even now much of it remains mysterious.

"You would be surprised if you ran across Charlie off-stage, for he is a completely different person to what you would expect," Ian Stewart once told me. "His hobby is studying the American Civil War. He has a collection of Civil War souvenirs that would be good enough for many a big museum. In a wardrobe hangs a complete uniform worn by a Confederate soldier. He has guns, items of clothing, buttons from tunics, and medals pinned to the wall. On his bookshelves are all the most authoritative books about that war . . . on one American tour, we had a week to spare so Charlie just vanished. We discovered later that he had been back to Gettysburg and all the other famous battlefields, and he walked round each one, picturing in his own mind how the troops had drawn themselves up for battle. "It was a terrible war," he told me afterwards. "So tragic—because it was between men who really had much in common. They should have been working together to build a country, not killing each other."

A *New Musical Express* feature once reported that Charlie's home had a fine library of books with authors ranging from Dylan Thomas to Oscar Wilde, many volumes on Art; that a green marble head of the Greek god Hypnos stood nearby; that in the bedroom he had a huge four poster bed with a sword rack at its head; that he had a special room for Shirley's collection of dolls; that his study was packed with rifles and revolvers from the American civil war. "Encased in glass is the Muster Roll for a troop of American cavalry which lists each man and his rank and how many dollars he drew in 1880. One trooper is recorded in small neat hand-writing as being executed for having stolen a rifle."

Once I got talking to Charlie about all this, a conversation that became quite animated when we discovered that we both bought books from the Bow Windows Book Shop in Lewes High Street. Charlie was talking about his copy of *The Groom's Oracle*, about a Bible he had that was printed in 1706, about a very old edition of *Foxe's Martyrs*, and volumes he had collected with illustrations by Arthur Rackham, then I took a note book out of my pocket—and the conversation stopped!

"No, I haven't got a marvellous collection of Civil War souvenirs. What made you think that?" he asked. "You saw it in a magazine, I suppose. I've got some guns, uniforms, a few bullets that were supposed to have been shot at the Battle of Little Big Horn—that's all . . . I love cowboy and indian stories," said Charlie. "Yes, I've got some nice books, with hand-coloured illustrations, but no-one wants to read about that, do they? You think so? Well, I don't! I've been collecting Georgian silver. But I don't want to talk about it. Who would be interested? It's very boring, isn't it? I've got some nice silver, but I've never paid more than £200 a piece for it. I like to find bargains in junk shops, and I don't just buy my stuff because it's *supposed* to be good—but because it *is* good. But nobody's interested in that, are they?"

In spite of this excessive modesty, which permeated every Charlie Watts interview as the Stones became successful (with reporters noting that he tried to stop his own photo being put on the cover of his first book, that he had none of his own paintings framed, etc), his qualities as a drummer were never under-rated.

The other Stones thought they were lucky to get him because good drummers are rare. And they were, because once he joined the group Charlie became their rhythmic binding force, underlining the bass of Bill Wyman, and driving the music along.

CHAPTER SIX

Bill Wyman was the last member to join the Rolling
Stones, and he did so by passing an audition at the
Weatherby Arms, a public house in the Kings Road,
Chelsea, after the group had advertised for a bass
guitarist in the weekly music paper *Melody Maker*.
Several things bothered him. "I didn't know whether
I should put my best suit on or not," he said afterwards.
Deciding on caution, Bill did dress up in his Sunday
best with a collar and tie—and arrived at the pub to
find Mick Jagger and Brian Jones standing at the bar,
long-haired and in jeans.

This was not the only contrast in life-style between
Bill and the two fledgling Stones—he was already a
married man with a settled way of life, a young son
to bring up, and he was eight years older than they
were! In retrospect, he seems to have been an unlikely
recruit.

In an interview with Richard Green of the *New
Musical Express* in May, 1964, Bill recalled: "I was
playing with a rock 'n' roll group in Penge before I saw
an advert for a bass guitarist with the Stones. I just
went along, practised with them and sat in for a few
numbers. We went through loads of tunes and messed
about a lot. It wasn't a real audition . . . they didn't
like me, but I had a good amplifier, and they were
badly in need of amplifiers at that time! So they kept
me on. Later, when they were going to get rid of me,

I think I clicked or something, and I stayed. I must have just fitted in."

Exactly how secure Bill was within the group in those early days, I could not say—but in October, 1965, rumours swept the music business that he was going to quit the Rolling Stones. When questioned by *Disc Weekly* about the rumours, Bill denied the allegations, said there had been no quarrels within the group, and that relationships couldn't be better. "It's the first I've heard of it," he said. "I don't know if any of the rest of the boys know about it. I'm certainly not quitting. If I'm thrown out I still get my money, but if I leave of my own accord, I don't. I'm not stupid," he said.

That was an understatement; Bill is a very canny lad—and has, like Charlie Watts, acquired a way of life and a breadth of interests way beyond those normally available to a musician.

Although this is not the date usually given in Rolling Stones press releases, Bill—whose real name is William Perks—was born on October 24th, 1936. He was brought up with two brothers, John and Paul, and two sisters, Judy and Anne, in Penge, Kent. Their father was a bricklayer and their mother worked at a factory bench.

His father, also called William Perks, used to play accordion on family outings, and down at the local pub, and he and his wife, Mrs. Kathleen Perks, encouraged all their children to take up musical instruments. By the time young Bill was fourteen years old, he was playing organ, piano and clarinet. "I remember telling them that if they learned to play an instrument, they would never be short of a pound," Mr. Perks once told the magazine *Today*.

Bill's piano lessons had started when he was four years old, and his mother once told me: "The trouble was he would never play at the right tempo, and was always messing around with the music. In the end, we got so fed up we gave the piano away . . . I can't remember him ever losing his temper. We found out later that when something annoyed Bill, he would go up to his bedroom and read the Bible—he was closely connected with our local church, and was a member of the choir for ten years, and was in line to become the church organist."

That ambition changed while Bill was in his late teens. He had gone to Beckenham Grammar School, and in that same interview with the *New Musical Express*, Bill recalled that when he left he "hadn't the faintest idea what I wanted to do. I didn't excel at anything, except Maths. Funny that, being good at Maths. I went to a firm in Lewisham and started as nothing in a little office job. I really was nothing. I got all the odds and ends that other people didn't want to do".

He spent his two years' National Service in the Royal Air Force, for the most part stationed in Germany; married his wife Diane in October, 1959 (they have since been divorced), and by the time he joined the Stones, Bill was making a career with the firm that had employed him when he first left school. He had left them once to work in a department store in Penge —but they later offered him an extra £3 a week to return to them, and he did. "I was soon in line for a good job," he said. 'There was one above me, then the manager. I had a good future, and they all asked me not to leave when I began to get on the Rolling Stones kick . . . even though I was playing with the Stones, I hadn't left the job. I was nearly dead, though. I'd be working with the Stones until 2 a.m., then I'd go home and have to be up again at 6 a.m. to go to the other place. Half the time, I didn't know where I was. So in the end I left the firm."

He and Diane had met at a dance at the Royston Ballroom, Beckenham, and went out together for eighteen months before they married—and it was early in 1960, some months after their wedding, that Bill started his own group, The Cliftons. In an interview with *Disc Weekly* in 1965, Diane said: "I was never particularly interested in pop music before Bill took it up. I'm still not particularly interested in it, although I like the Stones' music . . . I never did mind him playing in a group because even if I did there's nothing much you can do about it! You either take it or you leave it. Once Bill started playing a guitar you couldn't get him to put it down. About seven months after he joined the Stones they turned professional. I didn't really mind one way or the other. He was bringing home around the same money from the group when he started as he was before, so it was up to him. Bill never really had short hair, so I don't see any difference in him since he joined the Stones. It really upset me when, especially in the early days the boys were called 'Cavemen' and dirty. You don't spend hours washing and ironing shirts to have people turn round and call your husband dirty . . . he's always been a family man and he loves his son, Stephen, who's three. Stephen, in return, is a man's child and he really pines for Bill when he's away . . . Bill is kind and considerate, but he's definitely the boss in the house. My main thing in life is to keep out of the way. I never have wanted to get involved in the life of the group . . . it's almost like an ordinary job with Bill when he's playing within any distance from home. He goes out to work but when he comes home he doesn't bring the rest of the group with him."

In his childhood, in his teens and in his early years of marriage, Bill had a very ordinary life. His parents smile at any suggestion that he might have been a rebel. "Billy a rebel? Never," says his mother. "The most rebellious thing I can remember him doing was upset the opposition at cricket by switching from his left hand to his right when he batted or bowled. He's ambidextrous, you see . . . he had a good sense of humour and got up to all manner of things. I don't think anyone ever got the upper hand of him. I remember once he went to a dance with Diane, and was turned away because his trousers were too tight. So the next week Bill went along again wearing a fairly wide pair of trousers. They let him in all right, and the first thing he did was to go into the cloakrooms and take them off. Underneath were the ones he had worn the week before . . . he had been very keen to join a group ever since leaving school. When he met up with the other Stones we weren't too happy at first because he had a wife and baby to support, though all that was a secret at the time. We helped out a little, as it was a struggle at the beginning. Not that that did any harm. I always think it is a help if you have to struggle a bit at the start."

As the Stones became successful and the money started to flow in, Bill Wyman matured. He had always been interested in astronomy; now he started collecting books on the subject. He took up photography, acquiring expensive lenses and often vanishing for a few days into the West Country to study wild flowers and old houses. He joined a record club in Tennessee to build up a specialised collection of blues records—and started hunting out old seventy-eights to add to a collection that ranged far and wide over different generations of music, including Bach, Tchaikovsky and Mozart; Cole Porter and Rodgers and Hammerstein; all the original rock 'n' roll stars; modern and traditional jazz. He started building a poetry collection—and became the Rolling Stones 'official librarian', filing away all their press cuttings, early documents, photos, press releases, souvenirs, etc, with the intentention of one day writing his own book on the group's history.

As soon as he was financially able, he started moving up the property ladder—first to a modern flat over a garage in Penge; then to a £15,000 house on the Elmstead Wood Close estate near Beckenham, which he described as "one of those places with ivy up the walls and leaded windows. It's got oak panelling in the sitting room and the garden is nice and big with big hedges all round . . . it's one of those mock places built about 1920". There he had his own studio, lined with books and his collection of records. When a reporter commented on the fact that there seemed to be no musical instruments, Bill said: "Why should I? A bricklayer doesn't build walls when he's not working . . . I'm a family man, I suppose. I keep myself to myself. Mick and Keith are the only two members of the group who go around with each other. I'm about the only Stone who has the same relationship with friends I had before the group started."

Later, after he and Diane had separated, Bill acquired the sort of home that he had always dreamed of possessing—Gedding Hall, a Suffolk mansion built mainly during the reign of Henry VIII, surrounded by a moat and fourteen acres of gardens, and he also became Lord of the Manor of Gedding and Thormwoods, as though to the manner born.

CHAPTER SEVEN

And so the Rolling Stones had come together—Brian Jones the immature dreamer; Mick Jagger, whose parents thought he would become a politician; Keith Richard, fresh from art college; Charlie Watts, the designer with a similar art school background, and Old Bill Perks, the married man with a secure job and a home in suburbia who had always longed to be a musician. Here were five distinctly individual people forming one group; looking back, one has to admit that it was an unlikely combination.

Originally, there had been six of them but Ian Stewart had dropped out after Andrew Loog Oldham and Eric Easton signed the Stones to their first management contract, although Stewart still often sat in on piano and organ at their recording sessions, occasionally joined them for live TV shows (concealed behind a screen without the audience knowing he was there), and is to this day the group's road manager. "I joined before Charlie or Bill and when we wanted a new drummer, I suggested Charlie to Brian," Stewart told the *New Musical Express* in September, 1964. "I left because of one or two things, and the Stones stayed as just five blokes instead of six . . . I don't want to be pointed at in the street and get torn to pieces, so I'm better off like this."

Stewart once told me: "I was the second person to join, and was their pianist until Andrew Oldham thought I ought to fade into the back-ground, partly because my hair wasn't long enough. There was a very good reason for this; Bill and I were the only ones who were working and we just couldn't go round with long hair, or we would have got the sack. So I stayed on as road manager, though I still play piano on many Stones records—and they pay me a royalty."

Ian Stewart worked as a clerk in the export sales department for ICI (Imperial Chemical Industries), and he had two other indispensable roles to fulfill within the group—he had sold the shares that ICI had given him under a scheme to encourage share-ownership and worker-participation amongst the company's employees to buy a van so that he could drive the Rolling Stones to their club and ballroom gigs, and also because he had a telephone on his office desk, which enabled him to handle all the group's bookings in the very early days, advertising the number (VICtoria 4444 extension 747) in *Jazz News*.

"I used to do all the business of the Stones at work, and every fortnight at ICI we used to get circulars telling us not to make private calls during office time, so you can guess what happened when my boss found out the real truth about extension 747. I was called into his office and threatened with the sack. I have never had such an uncomfortable ten minutes in my life!"

As he drove the van and booked the gigs, Ian Stewart was right at the heart of the group's life; he travelled everywhere with them, knew them all intimately.

"I must admit being a Stone and also doing a day job was too much for me," he told me. "Sometimes, we wouldn't get home from a job until 3 or 4 a.m. in the morning, and then I would have only an hour or two in bed before going back to work again. Bill was in the same boat. Often I used to spend the night on a couch round at his place because I was just too tired to drive the rest of the journey home . . . there was a time when Bill nearly left the group because Diane felt he was not spending enough time at home. 'What sort of time do you think this is to come home?' she said to us as we rolled in the door. The other Stones, then all unmarried, were sympathetic. It was agreed that Bill would only play with us if the money was good. If it was bad, then he stayed at home . . . every night I used to call in at Edith Grove on my way home from work to pick up Mick, Keith and Brian so that we'd go on to a gig if we had one. At that time, they were starving, and Bill and I were buying them food with what little money was left out of our own wages . . . we had very few bookings partly because no-one wanted to book us, and partly because we wanted to rehearse before playing around the clubs, which were the big thing at that time.

"The truth was that we had had a row with officials of the National Jazz Federation. They thought we were a bunch of long haired scruffs, and were annoyed because wherever we appeared there had been noisy scenes whereas Alexis Korner and Cyril Davies only drew mild applause. They wanted groups with saxes and trumpets, but Mick, Keith and Brian weren't interested in mixing their Blues with the fashionable sort of jazz of Ray Charles and Cannonball Adderley. The boys would not be told by anyone how or what to play; it did not matter how important he was. There was quite a lot of jealousy behind it all, and the fact

58

that we were young—and rather big-headed, too—didn't help matters, either.

"We suspected at the time that even club owners were being asked not to book us. So, rather than be beaten, we decided to open our own club at South Oxhey, near Watford, where we hired a hall for the night for just a few shillings. We arrived right on time, tuned our instruments—and waited for the audience to arrive. They did—all *ten* of them! That night, our courage reached a very low ebb. We had had bad moments before. There were two evenings at Ealing —once when there was a foot of snow on the ground, and another time when there was a dense pea souper fog—when not a single person turned up.

"But that night at South Oxhey was different. The weather was fine, and we had booked the hall ourselves. There was nobody to blame but us. We knew the answer. It was simple; nobody wanted to see us.

"That night, Mick was beginning to regret that he had ever thrown up his economics course at the London School of Economics—and Dick Taylor told us that he had made up his mind. "My exams must come first," he said, and they did. That was his last night as a Rolling Stone. But the rest of us stayed together, and the turning point came when we persuaded Charlie to join us. He was already a minor star on the club circuit. Though he had broadcast several times with Alexis Korner, Charlie really wanted to change to another group. The reason was an obvious one—Charlie had a steady daytime job as a graphic designer, sometimes earning £50 a week. Korner was beginning to get more and more bookings out of town, and it was reaching the point where Charlie had to choose between a full-time job as an artist, or his life as a musician. He thought about it very carefully, and finally decided that there just wasn't enough money with Korner to justify throwing up his job. So he spent evenings as a Rolling Stone instead, and immediately became a close personal friend of Keith's; they have been bosom pals ever since."

One of the people who phoned Ian Stewart at his desk at ICI was Andrew Loog Oldham. He had then—early in 1963—just finished working with the Beatles, a job that had lasted five months after a chance meeting that he and they and their manager Brian Epstein had had on the set of *Thank Your Lucky Stars* in January, 1963, just before their first really big hit, *Please Please Me*. Andrew was already handling publicity for the singer Mark Wynter, and agreed to also look after the Beatles' publicity on a part-time basis. He gave the job up when Epstein decided the Beatles needed a full time press officer.

One evening Oldham was drinking in a pub in Shaftesbury Avenue with the music writer Peter Jones, who mentioned that he had seen the Stones at Richmond; then George Harrison mentioned the Rolling Stones and Oldham was sufficiently alert to follow up the hints—he phoned Ian Stewart and asked for their address, went round to see them at Edith Grove, and went down to Richmond to see them playing at the Station Hotel, where they now had this weekly booking at Giorgio Gomelski's Crawdaddy Club. As I mentioned in the first chapter, Gomelski regarded Brian Jones as the driving force behind the group—and it was Jones who kept pestering him for a written contract.

"If I had drawn up a contract, I suppose I might

have become a very rich man; but I never believe in these stupid bits of paper," Gomelski once told me.

Being an idealist at heart, Giorgio was saddened when the Rolling Stones left him. "I thought we had a verbal understanding, and I felt tremendously let down when they left me and signed up with Andrew Oldham. I was very upset by it. I think the Rolling Stones missed out by leaving me. I was sorry, yes—but I think they have much more reason to be sorry," he once told me. "If they had stayed with me, I think their work would have become more meaningful . . . I don't think they have grown up at all. They haven't grown up musically, and they haven't grown up as people. Certainly, they have not grown up as artists; they are still rising on a level of violence," said Gomelski (this was in 1968, though in my view little has happened in their career since to affect the validity of his comments).

"That was how they were at the very beginning. I suppose if they had stayed with me, I would probably have avoided them growing chips on their shoulders. Certainly, that's what they seem to have. But what are they rebelling against? I'm not against people rebelling . . . but it seems to me that with them it has become a gratuitous thing. They have neither the breadth or the width of talent that the Beatles have, though I think they have a great strength. A few of the things they have done like *Satisfaction* are classics of their kind. The rhythm there is hypnotic. But I don't want to work with monsters. Even if people are greatly talented, if they're monsters I don't want to work with them . . . the Stones were monsters and had this satanic power. They were inconsiderate and selfish, though perhaps they may have changed a little now. I very rarely see them now. Bill Wyman and Charlie Watts were always very beautiful people and very talented.

"Charlie was a very good graphic designer, and Bill used to work with the group often getting home at three or four o'clock in the morning, and then at eight o'clock he'd be at work. I used to admire him for that . . . Jones should have had treatment. His responses were never those of a normal person . . . Jagger was always very well organised and ambitious, but also selfish . . . and Keith was very spoilt. But, you know, they never had a hard time of it. They only had to rough it for six or eight months."

That was Giorgio Gomelski remembering his association with the Rolling Stones after the event; at the time he was glad to find a group to appear regularly at his Crawdaddy Club, and in an interview with the *New Musical Express* he said that before booking them he had long admired the Stones musically. "We had to find a group to play at the club at short notice. The Stones agreed to do the job very quickly on the promise of £1 a man for the first night. Actually, we did better than this—they got £7.50 between them and about 150 people turned up. But they never got less than this and by Easter things were healthy . . . I couldn't really offer them a contract. They hadn't even made a record then and I just couldn't afford it. I had a contract with them that was only verbal. It was the way I wanted to work. They had been approached by goodness knows how many people and eventually they went to Andrew Oldham and Eric Easton . . . I have a seven-minute documentary of the Rolling Stones still.

It was supposed to be a twenty-minute film but we never got round to finishing it. The Stones had left me by then. They sing *Pretty Thing* in the film and it shows them arriving at the club and all that . . . I took the tapes (of the soundtrack and background music) along to Decca and they turned them down."

But it was to be Decca who eventually did sign the Stones to a recording contract, though by then Andrew Oldham and Eric Easton were the group's managers. Decca were looking for a promising new group having already earned the unfortunate reputation for being the recording company that turned down The Beatles (though, to be fair to Decca, it should be said that they were not alone; there were other companies that also thought the Beatles would never make it—though their errors of judgement never became so public). Andrew Oldham had contacts at Decca, but like so many young entrepreneurs in the music business in the sixties he had very little capital of his own—which was where Eric Easton came into the picture. The Stones had made some recordings at the IBC studios and before they could sign with Decca, Oldham had to buy the IBC tapes—which meant raising the sum of £90. Oldham did not have the money—and Easton, who already had his own agency, did.

As I mentioned earlier, Oldham had phoned Ian Stewart at his desk at ICI. "Andrew asked if he could meet the Stones, and I told him their address in Edith Grove and he went along to see them," said Stewart. "By this time the Stones were receiving approaches from quite a number of people in the music business, but they liked Andrew. Like them he was young, ir-reverent, full of enthusiasm and eager to make a fortune. He was only nineteen at the time and had had little experience in the high pressure world of pop music. But there was no handicap as far as the Stones were concerned. A few days later he became their manager. Whenever we received any bad publicity, Andrew never worried—as long as our name was in the headlines."

The other key figures in the Stones' story at this time were The Beatles, who had always been naturally gregarious and felt lonely now that they were spending much of their time down in London, staying at the President Hotel in Russell Square, away from their usual haunts in Liverpool—the coffee bars and the Blue Angel Club where they had often spent much of their time drinking with other musicians when not working, or after a gig. Now, with their first records in the charts, they could not get back to Merseyside so easily. Their days in London were busy, but by late evening they had nowhere to go and few friends—and it was George Harrison who first heard of the Crawdaddy Club at Richmond, and the success that this new group were having there, the Rolling Stones.

The first night they went to Richmond was in either February or March, 1963, when Ian Stewart was still playing piano with the Stones. "In the interval, Mick, Keith and Brian stood chatting with them, and then afterwards we invited them back to Edith Grove, where we all sat talking and listening to records until nearly four o'clock, including some demos that the Stones had done, but which had never been issued. It was a bit of an eye-opener for the Beatles, who had been brought up on a completely different kind of music to the Stones," said Ian Stewart.

"I remember John Lennon was not very impressed by our treasured recordings of Jimmy Reed, which we had written away to America for because these albums were just unobtainable in this country. John and the other Beatles were all Tamla Motown fans at the time. They were wild about Chuck Jackson. As the evening went on the Beatles started to tell us stories about fans, and how they had been mobbed after different shows. Mick and Brian thought this was marvellous, and sat eagerly gulping down their mugs of coffee. "That's great—that'll happen to us one day," said Mick.

"Just before they left—I drove George and Ringo back to the President—John invited us to a show they were appearing in some weeks later at the Royal Albert Hall. It was a big BBC concert. To avoid having to buy tickets, the Stones walked in the back door, carrying the Beatles' guitars . . . after that the boys often went around with the Beatles. At first we were rather big time about it. Mick and Brian were really proud to think they were close friends of Britain's leading pop stars.

"One night we all went to the Marquee, the Soho club where the Stones had made their debut the previous summer deputising for one night for Alexis Korner. Everybody knew them there. Mick and Brian were buying everyone bottles of Coke—as though they had all the money in the world. The truth was that we were just as broke as ever, and literally had only a few pennies left in our pockets at the end of the evening. But at least Brian thought we had made a good impression on the Beatles!

"At that time they were so fed up with living in

hotels that John wanted the Beatles to move in with Mick, Keith and Brian in Edith Grove. Nothing came of that, but the Beatles were constantly encouraging us in every way they could."

Gomelski has similar memories of this same period: "I remember when the Beatles were appearing at the Albert Hall, Brian was mistaken for a Beatle as he walked in the stage door, and was mobbed. He loved it. He told me afterwards, 'Giorgio, it was a lovely feeling—that's how I want it to be'. Of course, the Beatles had been to watch the Stones at Richmond and thought the group was wonderful. Many times John and Paul came back to my flat for soup and omelettes, talking with the Stones about music into the early hours."

By then, the Stones had already received their first newspaper coverage—a feature in the local paper in Richmond, *The Richmond and Twickenham Times*, written by Barry May who later became a music writer. Brian Jones was so delighted with the fact that they were now in print that he carried a cutting of the story around in his wallet for many months afterwards; I still have the cutting in my own files, and now over eleven years later it's fascinating to see how the Stones appeared at the time: "A musical magnet is drawing the jazz beatniks away from Eel Pie Island, Twickenham, to a new mecca in Richmond. The attraction is the new Craw-Daddy Rhythm and Blues Club at the Station Hotel, Kew Road—the first club of its kind in an area of flourishing modern and traditional jazz haunts . . . from a meagre 50 or so on the club's first night, less than two months ago, attendances have rocketed by an average of 50 a week to last Sunday's record of 320. And the membership book lists more than 700 names of rhythm and blues devotees from all parts of London and West Surrey . . . the Rollin' Stones, a six-piece group, were formed just ten months ago. Since then they have played in more than a dozen London rhythm and blues clubs, as well as appearances at the West End Marquee Club . . . although "pop" numbers are sometimes played, songs written and recorded by the American rhythm and blues guitarist Bo Diddley are the Rollin' Stones' favourites. Their appreciation of him is carried to the extent of naming the club after a dance Bo Diddley has invented, the "craw-daddy". The 300 and more in their late teens and early twenties who pack the club on Sunday nights do a dance similar to the craw-daddy. But most improvise on a wildly remote form of the hully-gully similar to the twist. For those less inclined to express their feelings for the music physically, the Rollin' Stones also provide visual entertainment.

"Hair worn Piltdown-style, brushed forward from the crown like the Beatles pop group—we looked like this before they became famous—the rhythm section, piano, drums and bass guitar, provide a warm, steady backing for the blues of the harmonica and lead guitars. Save for the swaying forms of the group on the spotlit stage, the room is in darkness. A patch of light from the entrance doors catches the sweating dancers and those who are slumped on the floor where chairs have not been provided . . ."

It was in this atmosphere that the Beatles first saw them, that Andrew Oldham and Eric Easton first heard them, that Giorgio Gomelski first filmed them. It was here that they came together in their final form, that the first part of their careers ended and the second began.

CHAPTER EIGHT

When Andrew Loog Oldham and Eric Easton first saw the Rolling Stones together down at the Station Hotel, they moved fast. They went down to Richmond together on April 28th, 1963. On May 3rd, they signed the group to a management and agency contract. Then they started negotiating with Decca. On May 10th, Oldham took the Stones into the Olympic studios and recorded their first tracks, *Come On* and *I Wanna Be Loved*. And on June 7th, the tracks were released as the Stones' first single on the Decca label—and that same day the Rolling Stones made their TV debut on the ABC TV programme *Thank Your Lucky Stars*.

Even to this days, few other managers have hustled with that speed. But Oldham's confidence matched the Stones' ambition; they deserved each other. Oldham recalled his trip to Richmond in an interview with *New Musical Express*. "I was probably forty-eight hours ahead of the rest of the business in getting there. But that's the way God planned it," he said.

He was just what the Stones needed; an arch-hustler. And he also had an unusual history of his own. He had been expelled from Wellingborough public school, had been gaoled in France for vagrancy and according to a feature in *Record Mirror*: "Andrew's family has no show business background and he received no training. His first, short job was as a tea boy at Hardy Amies' fashion house, which explains the passion for clothes that gripped him until recently." 'I liked wearing good clothes. They were important when I had no money because they attracted attention and helped me to become noticed in show business. But I've realised that once you have made it, people don't like to see you well dressed—they think it's flashy, I suppose.' After a few months in the fashion world Andrew set off for the South of France where he became a con man—invaluable experience for learning how to handle people. "I lived off English tourists. I approached them using a public school accent and said: 'Excuse me, Sir, I wonder if you could help me. I've run out of money and can't get a job because I haven't been able to get a work permit. My mother would be worried sick if I wrote to her for money. I'm getting a permit in the next few days but meanwhile could you lend me ten francs?' The tourists loved it, particularly the upper class people. I was just seventeen years old and pulling in £8 a day, living in Cannes, Juan-les-Pins and St. Tropez. Sometimes I'd run into my benefactors in night clubs but they were too drunk to recognise me! I stayed on the Riviera for eight months, went to jail briefly for vagrancy. On the whole, I found it dead easy and felt like Cary Grant in a comedy."

In another interview, this time with the *Sunday Mirror*, Oldham was described as "a long haired gangling youth who uses make-up and swears like a dyspeptic drill sergeant. Some say he is as mad as a five-bob watch. Others acclaim him as a genius of pop". He was then sharing a flat with the Stones, and explained: "My mother kicked me out. I turned up on their doorstep saying would they take me in. It was very funny considering I was their manager." He also said he had been to a psychiatrist: "At group therapy

I listened to a bloke telling us how frightened he was to kiss his girl-friend because he had acne. I didn't have time to listen to the others. It was all very funny." And he opined that the reason why he wore dark glasses day and night was "maybe to withdraw behind them into myself".

But for all his oddness, Andrew Loog Oldham knew his rock 'n' roll, knew a good sound when he heard it, and was a hard-driving opportunist. When asked in that *New Musical Express* interview what it was that had first excited him about the Rolling Stones when he saw them in Richmond, he said: "Music. Sex. The fact that in just a few months the country would need an opposite to what the Beatles were doing. I remember seeing the Beatles in Doncaster when they were about eighth on the bill to people like Helen Shapiro and Tommy Roe. I sat there with a lump in my throat. In just one night you knew they were going to be very big. It was just an instinctive thing. From that night on it registered subconsciously that when they made it, another section of the public were gonna want an opposite. The Stones were gonna be that opposite. That's the way it worked out. In the early days, the way that the media was running, was that you could invite the Beatles in for tea, but you couldn't invite the Stones . . . certain people claimed to be managing them, but I never saw any contracts. As far as I'm concerned, they didn't have a manager. So we went ahead and cut the first record *Come On*. We did it on a four-track. I'd never produced a record before and the engineer turned round to me at the end of the session and said: 'What about mixing it?' I said: 'What's that?' He looked at me like I was a real dummy

71

and slowly explained. I just shrugged: 'Oh, you do that. I'll come back in the morning.'

"My first jobs were to hustle for a decent recording contract and gigs. I went everywhere with them. There were a couple of compromises that had to be made first. Someone even said we would have to get rid of the lead singer because he would never pass a BBC audition. For the first *Thank Your Lucy Stars* appearance—just to get them on with the first record— we compromised to the extent of wearing some sort of uniform. We knew we had to . . . if the Stones had dressed the way they wanted, they wouldn't have been allowed inside the building. So they all wore those checked jackets. But we got rid of them as soon as we could."

So remembered Andrew Loog Oldham long after the event, but nearer the time the Rolling Stones never seemed all *that* different to me—and in no sense outrageous. They wore their hair no longer than many students. Their clothes were not particularly non-conformist—even in their own press photos they were seen wearing collars and ties, or black turtle neck sweaters with sports jackets. Frequently, different members of the group wore well cut City-style suits. In their press releases (three of these are reproduced in the appendices to save space), they were just as forthcoming in giving the personal details that young fans always like to have as any other pop group—saying what they weighed, how tall they were, and giving the colour of their hair and eyes, their parents' names and those of their brothers and sisters, and their personal choice of colours, food, drink and clothes.

The truth is that for all the later attempts to glorify

the group, to elevate their social significance, and to analyse their success, the Rolling Stones started off as just another pop group. Unlike the Beatles, they did not write their own material—and were no more or less important than Billy J. Kramer and the Dakotas, The Searchers, The Hollies and The Mojos. What was distinctive about them was their musical roots—which were in rhythm and blues rather than rock 'n' roll. Musically, even then they were superlative, playing as well on stage as they did in the recording studio. But they were just as anxious as all the other groups of their day to have their photos in the teenage magazines, to reply to their fan mail, to assist their fan club (yes, they had one), and to get their records in the hit parade.

But all this took rather longer to happen than Andrew Oldham had expected. That first single was not the huge success that he thought it would be, and only entered the lower regions of the charts; their next single *I Wanna Be Your Man* only made eight or nine in the charts, and in that *New Musical Express* interview, Oldham said their career did not really start to gather momentum until the release of *Not Fade Away* in February, 1964, by which time the Beatles had already had four No. 1 singles. "Although it was a Buddy Holly song, I considered it to be like the first song Mick and Keith 'wrote'," said Oldham. "They picked the concept of applying that Bo Diddley thing to it. The way they arranged it was the beginning of the shaping of them as songwriters. From then on they wrote . . . the common ground we shared was that we knew as little as each other. We just had a basic desire to do something: a hustling instinct."

It was those other hustlers, the Beatles, who gave their career its biggest boost. They had just been to collect their Variety Club of Great Britain awards from the Prime Minister, Harold Wilson, and John Lennon and Paul McCartney were travelling back through the West End by taxi. They saw Oldham walking down the street, stopped the taxi, gave him a lift—and told him they had written a song, *I Wanna Be Your Man*, which was just right for the Stones. Oldham told them the group was rehearsing at Studio 51 in Soho—and they re-routed the taxi, went straight round there, and played the number over.

Although their singles were not achieving the immediate success that Oldham had initally expected, the Rolling Stones were fast developing an image that was all their very own—helped along by national press stories about their long hair and rebellious attitudes, and a long series of trivial disputes between the Stones and people ranging from TV producers to an airline hostess, to hotel and restaurant managers and even a garage attendant, plus the occasional brush with the law, and publicity master-strokes like the headline WOULD YOU LET YOUR DAUGHTER MARRY A ROLLING STONE? In their private lives, the Stones were just as sane, civilised and conventional as any other group of predominantly middle class people of their own age, but their public image was rapidly becoming the very opposite: they were portrayed as long haired, scruffy, dirty, unwashed, foul-mouthed, vulgar, immoral, thick, inarticulate and incoherent—and they appeared to do little to dispel the general impression.

This was an image largely created for them by the

national press, who had never really understood pop music, and who had the suspicion that every event within the music business was a stunt. But the Stones' clashes with minor symbols of authority were not stunts. Oldham was shrewd enough to realise that the age of the organised pop music stunt was very nearly over. Having been a publicist and having helped to launch the Beatles, he understood that to be successful you had to project yourself. In that *New Musical Express* interview, he explained: "None of those things the Stones got up to were stunts." And when asked whether it was a case of the press picking up the smallest things and saying 'The Wild Men Strike Again', Oldham said that was: "Right. Thank God for the media. Except for the compromises they made early on, the Stones could just be themselves and that was sufficient to become what they are now." Asked whether there was a feeling of amusement within the Stones' circle at the way people reacted to them, Oldham said: "Yes, there was. Like on the German tour someone said to Mick that it would be really hysterical if he did the goose-step during the instrumental break in *Satisfaction*. Well, Jagger being Jagger not only does that, he goes on stage and does the whole Hitler routine. The audience were going crazy anyway and that just drove them berserk. There were too many fuzz and dogs in the theatre for them to do anything then, but when they got outside they overturned a hundred and thirty cars and every train leaving the city for the suburbs was wrecked completely . . ."

But their press coverage did not start off like that; when *Come On* crept into the charts at the beginning of August, 1963, their interviews in the music papers were just as mundane as those given by any other artist of the time. "The Rolling Stones first burst into prominence as the long-haired London group with a twitch that was a kind of dance, who appeared on *Thank Your Lucky Stars* recently," reported the *New Musical Express* on August 2. "Says Mick Jagger, lead vocal and harmonica with the Stones: 'The twitch business really comes from a regular club session we do at Richmond, near London. It gets so crowded that all the fans can do is stand and twitch. They can't dance because there isn't room. We picked it up from there.' "

Then later in the month, the paper reported again that: "The Rolling Stones is a London group with the Liverpool sound, according to some. Rhythm-and-blues fans say they are the only British combo which bears comparison with American r-and-b units. Their own opinion is simply that they are unique. Spokesman Brian Jones, who sings and plays harmonica (sic), says: 'We believe that we sound like ourselves and no-one else.' They are, they claim, first and foremost a rhythm and blues group. If you refer to them as a beat outfit, they frown. If you venture to suggest that they play rock 'n' roll, they positively glower. In appearances on stage they seem to resemble long-haired dervishes . . . they believe in complete individuality and free expression. Not that they are beatniks. They aren't! Their music reflects this freedom. All keen r-and-b fans, they started off playing solid, earthy Muddy Waters stuff. Lately, though, their repertoire has in-cluded more generally popular material by people like Chuck Berry and the Drifters . . . 'I suppose you could say we've made some concessions,' says Mick Jagger, lead vocalist and harmonica, 'but we still play what we like. We consider ourselves professional-amateurs. We still have the enthusiasm to treat the business as an enjoyable pastime, but also the professionalism to realise that you can't turn up late for dates and that sort of thing.' "

The now-defunct magazine *Hit Parade* reported: "In these hectic days of Liverpool chart domination it has become almost an event for any group outside Merseyside to break into the hit lists, but that is just what the London-based Rolling Stones did with their version of the Chuck Berry number, *Come On*. 'To be perfectly frank, we were a little surprised ourselves when the record got into the charts,' says Brian Jones, the group's leader. 'For a time it is hard to associate yourself with the disc when you hear it played on the radio. I suppose you get over this kind of thing in time, but at the moment we are fresh enough to the business to enjoy all the little kicks.' . . . A couple of weeks ago, they took a trip to the famed Liverpool Cavern Club, and in Mick Jagger's own words: 'It was all the gear. They really seemed to reckon us. We went there just to have a dance and relax. We had done a show in Manchester earlier that evening, and so were in the Cavern just for pleasure. But when the word got about that we were in the place, we didn't stop signing autographs all night.' "

Meanwhile, their live appearances were reaching a different level. They started moving away from the smaller clubs and ballrooms and began making theatre tours, instead—making an autumn tour with Bo Diddley and the Everly Brothers; another in January with the Ronettes and Marty Wilde, and then a third in February with John Leyton. But perhaps the most important development was their association with Gene Pitney for whom Mick Jagger and Keith Richard wrote *That Girl Belongs To Yesterday*, which gave him a major US hit before the two songwriting Stones had ever written any material for their own group. Pitney also went along to the studios where the Rolling Stones were recording—and so did the American producer Phil Spector, who had been the most influential producer of the Fifties making such classics as the Teddy Bears' *To Know Him Is To Love Him* (which he also wrote, taking the line from his father's tombstone) and then *He's A Rebel* and *Then He Kissed Me* by the Crystals, and *Be My Baby* and *Baby, I Love You* by the Ronettes and who later—in the mid-Sixties—went on to produce two of the best records of the decade *You've Lost That Loving Feeling* by the Righteous Brothers and *River Deep, Mountain High* by Ike and Tina Turner.

Spector went along to that Rolling Stones session as a friend—both of them and their producer/manager, Andrew Oldham, and also of Pitney. He was not the producer; Oldham was. But out of that session came their next single *Not Fade Away/Little By Little*. The A-side was a revival of an old Buddy Holly number, which Oldham thought marked the beginning of the Jagger-Richard songwriting partnership; they gave it that Bo Diddley rhythm and blues 'feel'. They were the best recordings the Stones had ever done—and were helped by Gene Pitney playing piano on *Little By Little*, which Jagger wrote with Spector, who played maraccas on both tracks. When the single was released, *The New Musical Express* reviewer said:

"Can't see the Rolling Stones missing out with their latest Decca release—a quivering, pounding rhythmic opus titled *Not Fade Away*. It's a solo voice showcase, but the backing beat is quite fantastic, with handclaps and wailing harmonica adding to the effect. That fascinating plaintive quality peculiar to all Norman Petty-Buddy Holly numbers is prominent, despite the raucous treatment. I would have preferred that the ending, unlike the title, did not fade away—but this minor detail won't prevent the boys from enjoying a big hit. Pungent, strident guitar work—ably assisted by Gene Pitney's tinkling piano—are showcased in Phil Spector's composition *Little By Little*. The melody is insignificant, but the sound's sensational."

That single established the Rolling Stones. In my view, it is still one of the best recordings they have done; it went to No. 3 in the charts, and spent nine weeks in the hit parade. And with its success, they developed from a group with a cult following to one with mass appeal. When they began their tour with John Leyton, the *New Musical Express* reported:

"Welcomed by a tremendous barrage from boys and girls alike, the Stones opened with *Talkin' 'Bout You*, but it was almost lost in the noise from the fans, who quietened down for Mick Jagger's harmonica break in *Road Runner* which followed. The group's guitar noise came far nearer the Chuck Berry original on *Roll Over Beethoven* than the Beatles do on record. The five, who are a visual as well as vocal act, then gave a tremen-

dous, terrific r-and-b work-out on Rufus Thomas'
Walking The Dog (again nearly all drowned by
fans). The screams did not let up for the slower
You'd Better Move On or *I Wanna Be Your Man*,
with which the caveman-like quintet ended."

Soon, the Rolling Stones were a nationwide phenomenon just like their friends The Beatles had been for the
past year. When the Stones' first album was released
by Decca in April, it went straight to No. 1 in the LP
charts—the first week in twelve months that The
Beatles had not ocupied that space. Within a fortnight,
the album sold over 150,000 copies.

And it was then that their managers Andrew Oldham
and Eric Easton pulled a master-stroke. Even though
the Rolling Stones had never had a major US hit, and
were still largely unknown outside Britain, they booked
the group into Carnegie Hall, New York.

CHAPTER NINE

It may seem strange now that rock music has become such an important part of the world's entertainment, but back in 1964 for the Rolling Stones to be booked to appear at Carnegie Hall was a major event within the music business. For ten years, American artistes had dominated the British charts; now the situation was reversed—and just a few months before the Beatles had made their first US tour. In February, 1964, the Beatles had become the first beat group ever to appear at Carnegie Hall.

By this one booking, the impression was suddenly created that the Rolling Stones were as important as the Beatles, even though they had only just had this first hit in Britain, and had never had one in the States.

As their plans took shape, Oldham and Easton soon had the Stones booked into other venues, too. It had already been announced that the Stones were to star in a major film that was to be produced by Lionel Bart and partly financed by Peter Sellers (a project that fizzled out). Now, it was announced that as well as appearing at Carnegie Hall the Stones would record a spot on the *Hollywood Palace* TV show on June 5th before appearing in concert at San Bernadino, Portland, Vancouver, Omaha, Flint, Chicago, Indianapolis, Philadelphia, Newhaven and Harrisburg, with Murray the K—disc jockey who had done so much to popularise the Beatles in the States—introducing their Carnegie Hall and Newhaven concerts.

By now the Stones had an image that far-exceeded their actual success, and when they appeared in concert with Peter and Gordon at East Ham Granada, London, fifty policemen were on duty, and a squad of first aid attendants to help the girls who were expected to faint (they did). Richard Green reported in the *New Musical Express*: "After the fantastic reception given to the Stones, it became even more obvious that they are approaching the Beatles' popularity and could even overtake the Mersey group. From my third row seat I had to lip-read on many occasions to find out what song was being performed! The screams from the audience completely drowned the Stones for long periods. The long-haired-ones began with *Beautiful Delilah* and were met with a torrent of gifts which plummeted on to the stage from all parts of the theatre. To their credit the Stones carried on even though they were hit several times. *Walking The Dog* followed, then another track from their LP *I Just Wanna Make Love To You*. The Stones were at their best and when they could be heard, they were churning out a great sound. Mick's dancing was grade one and served to incite fresh attacks of frenzy from the fans. Even though *You Better Move On* is a slow number, the screams continued but you should have heard what happened during *I'm Alright*. From the moment Mick picked up his maraccas and the Stones burst into action it was a battle between them and the teenagers as to who could make the most noise . . . it was over ten minutes after the act finished before the fans stopped chanting *We Want The Stones*."

Immediately after that concert, the Stones left for the States—and apart from their concerts, they also began recording at the Chess studios in Chicago where

Muddy Waters, Chuck Berry and Bo Diddley had cut many of their own albums. There, the Stones cut four numbers including their next single *It's All Over Now* —but they were advised not to go down to the South Side area of Chicago where all the rhythm and blues clubs were because of the racial tensions. It wasn't a wholly successful tour. Bill Wyman wrote back to the *New Musical Express* that: "We did a date in Minneapolis which was organised only two days before. Nobody had heard of us. I think the reaction was the same as we first experienced in England a year ago— complete disbelief and curiosity. There weren't many people there because the tickets were three dollars." And when they appeared at San Antonio in Texas, a *Daily Mirror* reporter wrote that: "Britain's Rolling Stones got 'the bird' when they appeared in a show at San Antonio, Texas, last night. Local singers were cheered wildly. A tumbling act and a trained monkey were recalled to the stage for encores. But the long-haired Rolling Stones—Mick Jagger, Keith Richard, Brian Jones, Charlie Watts and Bill Wyman—were booed. After the show, at the Teen Fair of Texas, one seventeen-year-old girl said: 'All they've got that our own school groups haven't is hair.' Only three thousand of the twenty thousand seats were filled. The Stones had to compete with several other attractions—including a rodeo show."

That Chicago-recorded single *It's All Over Now* gave the Stones their first Number One hit. They also brought out an EP *Five By Five*, and by the end of July were being followed by teenage riots wherever they appeared in Britain just as the Beatles had been. When they turned up at the Rediffusion TV studios in Kingsway to appear on *Ready, Steady, Go!* twenty policemen on foot plus more on motorbikes tried to control the teenage mob outside the studio—and a car door was wrenched off as the Stones were driven away by their chauffeur. "It was one of the most horrifying mobbings we've ever had," said Jagger. Then at the Winter Gardens, Blackpool, police made a baton charge into the crowd as an angry mob began breaking up the place. "A group of youths kept spitting at us while we were playing. I lost my temper and tried to kick one of them," said Keith Richard. In the ensuing riot, amplifiers, drums and other equipment worth more than £1,000 were smashed as youths clambered over the stage, ripping down the red and gold velvet curtains. Two policemen and thirty fans were injured. Later, four youths appeared in court charged with assault and carrying offensive weapons. "It was terrifying," said Brian Jones. And Blackpool's Deputy Chief Constable Mr. Ronald Gregory said: "We shall advise the Winter Gardens authorities that they must not have the Rolling Stones again."

When they appeared at Belle Vue, Manchester, more than a hundred girls fainted—and so did two policewomen, one of them having to be taken to hospital with suspected rib fractures. At the Tower Ballroom, New Brighton, thirty four bouncers guarded the stage and the *Daily Express* reported: "The bouncers work swiftly, ruthlessly and non-stop, dealing with girls in fits and girls in faints. Some of the girls in fits are violent. They fight their way screaming on to the low stage and fight to get up to the Rolling Stones. Girls come spinning, reeling off the low stage, laughing, crying, coming round slowly, it seems from some anaesthetic."

Charlie Watts told *Disc*: "Sure, there's a lot of screaming and that. They scream because we're popular, I think, and because they want to let us know it. They get excited, too, and so do we when we're playing to 'em. It's the atmosphere, you know. Gets all hot and sticky, and everybody's having a great time. Riot's the wrong word. Enthusiasm is more like it . . . the faints and the shovings only started happening regularly since the newspapers started writing about riots."

It was no surprise when the Rolling Stones were voted Britain's most popular group in the annual *Melody Maker* poll in September. By now starting to have a growing international following, the Stones started appearing regularly in France, Holland, Belgium and Germany—though they turned down an offer to appear in South Africa because of that Government's apartheid policy. In October, they had their first US hit with *Time's On My Side*—and that same month began their second US tour with a concert at the New York Academy of Music. In November, they brought out another Number One single *Little Red Rooster*, written by Willie Dixon, which had advance orders of 300,000.

By now, controversy was following them everywhere. In *The News of the World*, Alan Whittaker wrote: "There are few mothers who wouldn't welcome a Beatle into the family. The Beatles bubble with laughter. They make jokes, wear neat clothes, get along with royalty. Even long hair becomes acceptable after a time. But it's different with the Stones. They leer rather than smile. They don't wear natty clothes. They glower. Nobody would accuse them of radiating charm. And the extraordinary thing is that more and more youngsters are turning towards the Stones. The Beatles have become too respectable. The five Stones—and their young manager, Andrew Oldham—are symbols of a rebellion against authority, against the boss, the clock, the clean-shirt-a-day routine. How true is this carefully-nourished picture of five indolent morons? The Stones give one the feeling that they really enjoy wallowing in a swill-tub of their own repulsiveness. They flick ash everywhere. Charlie Watts, the zombie-eyed drummer, has a habit of dropping cigarette ends in other people's coffee cups—before they've finished drinking."

And of Andrew Oldham, he wrote: "He has an odd sort of humour. At Paris airport he suddenly collapsed into a fake faint. When people rushed to help him he jumped up and cackled. At Brussels airport he pretended to be a cripple having difficulty walking down a staircase. When the plane taking the Stones from Brussels to Paris took off, he called out: 'I hope everyone realises the pilot is a spastic.'"

After the Rolling Stones appeared on the Ed Sullivan show in the States, Sullivan told an American paper: "I promise you they'll never be back on our show." This was after teenagers in the audience had rioted. "If things can't be handled, we'll stop the whole business," said Sullivan. "We won't book any more rock 'n' roll groups and we'll ban teenagers from the theatre if we have to. Frankly, I didn't see the group until the day before the broadcast. They were recommended to me by my scouts in England. I was shocked when I saw them . . . it took me seventeen years to build this show. I'm not going to have it destroyed in a matter of weeks."

Before the Rolling Stones arrived in Milwaukee for a concert, the Mayor was interviewed on radio—and described their concert as "an immoral thing for teen-agers to be able to exhibit themselves at", and when they visited Cleveland, the Mayor there told the local newspaper: "Such groups do not add to the community's culture or entertainment."

Back in Britain, the Stones were involved in another dispute—this time with the BBC. It started when they failed to turn up for two recording sessions for the radio programmes *Top Gear* and *Saturday Club*. Mick Jagger said afterwards: "I understand that the bookings were made on our behalf, but we never consented to them. That is partly the reason we didn't turn up." Then Mick Jagger appeared in court again at Tettenhall, Staffordshire, accused of three more motoring offences. At this time his solicitor, Mr. Dale Parkinson, told the magistrates: "Put out of your mind this nonsense talked about these young men. They are not long-haired idiots but highly intelligent university men. The Duke of Marlborough had much longer hair than my client, and he won some famous battles. His hair was powdered, I think because of fleas—my client has no fleas! The Emperor Caesar Augustus was another with rather long hair. He won many great victories. Long hair is worn by barristers in court curled up at the ends . . . this unhappy country suffers from a perennial disease called the balance of payments crisis and it needs every dollar it could earn. The Rolling Stones earn more dollars than many professional exporters."

Then the group themselves were involved in another controversy when ABC TV organised a party for them —and they did not turn up. "We knew nothing about this reception," said Mick Jagger afterwards. They also refused to attend a photographic session to have their pictures taken with Petula Clark.

The disputes (which would have been bad news for any other group) seemed constant—they were forever being refused admission to hotels and restaurants; were said to have reduced an airline hostess to tears; Mick, Bill and Brian were each fined £5 for insulting behaviour after urinating against a filling station wall, and a Glasgow magistrate described the Rolling Stones as "animals, clowns and morons" when one of their fans was arrested for breaking a window—prompting two Members of Parliament to defend the group.

"Mind you, I will admit that some of the bad publicity was deserved," Ian Stewart told me, adding that: "Andrew Oldham never worried—as long as our name was in the headlines! There was a time when we were banned by Associated Television for turning up late for *The Arthur Haynes Show*. We were two hours late for the rehearsal itself, and it seemed clear to us that our kind of music was not suited to this type of TV show. Our hearts were just not in it. When the rehearsal was over Mick and Keith turned to me and said: 'We want to go and get some clothes.' I told them there was no time, but they said: 'Oh, to hell with this lot. We're going off.' So I went with them down to Carnaby Street where we browsed in the mod shops for an hour or so, until I reminded Mick that the final run-through was about to begin. 'There's plenty of time for that,' he said. 'Let's go and have some tea.'

So we all did. By the time we reached ATV studios the producer was going berserk, and we were nearly an hour and a half late again. The bigwigs at ATV were so annoyed that they told us we could never appear on any of their shows again. Of course, now that the Stones are a world attraction, second only to the Beatles, they have had to change their minds!

"The Stones have been banned so often that it gets monotonous," Stewart continued. "We have been banned by hotels because of our long hair; refused meals in restaurants because we have not worn ties—and have even been banned by a major airline, British United Airways. That all blew up one day when we were touring the Channel Islands, and were due to fly from Jersey to Guernsey. At Jersey airport, we were climbing up the steps to our plane when the air hostess said in a stage whisper: 'Well, boys have you washed today?'

"That is the sort of comment that really annoys the Stones. But though she could see that they were all angry, she did not let it rest at that. Instead, she added: 'When did you last have your hair cut?' That was it. The boys let rip, tore into her quite mercilessly—and kept asking for drinks, coffee and cigarettes so that she was kept running up and down the plane, and they kept criticising her, christening her Hilary Hedgehopper. By the time the plane reached Guernsey thirty minutes later, she was in tears. She had never had to face such an outburst of abuse in her life, and it was more than she could take. She was sobbing. Naturally, as always happens, the authorities assumed she was right and we were wrong.

"The result was inevitable. We were told we could

never fly BUA again. Not that that worried us. We don't like their planes in any case! Brian said afterwards that we should have bought the airline to teach them a lesson!

"Unless you had been with the Stones you would never believe the insults we have to face from people prejudiced just because they happen to have long hair, and dress unorthodoxly. Everybody seems to suspect the worst—particularly parents who think their daughters are never safe when there is a Rolling Stone around. Even the police suspect us, though they have to protect us. They know now that whenever the Stones visit a town there will be riots. There always are. There always have been.

"There was one night in Bournemouth when we had terrible trouble because the local police had been warned that two young girls of thirteen had run away from their homes in the North of England, telling their families they were going to see the Stones. Every girl we spoke to that day was approached by the police, who followed us wherever we went—and even back to our hotel after the show. There was quite a rumpus when the police discovered that one Stone had gone back to the hotel with a girl. They got the manager out of bed, and marched into the hotel. But that was soon settled. She was not one of them. And in any case, she was over sixteen! Brian invited the police to join us in the lounge for coffee. While we were sitting there —it was two o'clock by this time—the Chief Inspector himself arrived, so we invited him to have coffee and sandwiches as well. By that time, everyone was friendly —and then in through the door walked one of the girls on the arm of our other road manager. All hell let loose! But the police, soon realising she hadn't been in any danger, just whisked her back home to her parents. After all, he wasn't to know who she was.

"Girls have always been a problem for the Stones, though the worst riots have involved boy fans, funnily enough. There were terrible scenes in Berlin, in Dublin and in Belfast, but I think the worst ever was at Scheningen in Holland.

"On the Continent, you often find that the keenest pop fans are boys. They like to dance together. While the Stones were playing two young kids jumped up on stage and started to dance. Then more came forward. At that moment, the police moved in and started throwing them off. Fighting broke out. Before we knew what had happened, everyone was battling it out in the theatre. The only thing to do when a fight breaks out in a ballroom is to carry on playing. If you stop, the real fans get resentful, and even out of hand. Sometimes, particularly in America, the police will try to stop a show. If they do, there is always far more trouble.

"On this occasion in Holland, the police formed a chain like fire-fighters. As soon as another teenager came forward, he was passed along the line, thumped as he went past, and then thrown out of the door and down some steps, where there were more policemen waiting to help him on his way. I have never seen police so vicious as they were that night in Holland, though the ones with least ideas when it comes to controlling crowds are the Americans.

"The Stones realise that the police have to be firm —but in America everyone is so litigation-happy that you only have to push a girl and you are liable to be threatened with a law suit. Some of our worst scenes have been caused because the American police have stood by, allowing fans to riot. The sort of thing that happens is this. You warn them in advance that there will be a concert on such and such a night. 'There will be trouble,' you tell them. 'Don't give us that, buddy,' they drawl. 'We've had the Beatles here—and we know how to control a crowd!' Of course, come the night of the show and there are nowhere near enough police. Then an emergency call goes out and they all start coming at once, revolvers strapped to their hips.

"One night in Los Angeles there were hundreds of girls blocking the exit to a theatre where we played. I asked them to get out of the way so that I could back the car up to the stage door, but they wouldn't—so I got into the car, and started moving slowly backwards towards them. Anywhere else, the girls would have just jumped out of the way. That is what would happen in Britain, Sweden, Holland or Australia. But not in America. Immediately, a burly police sergeant, two guns hanging from his belt, stormed over. 'You just stop that, boy,' he warned me. 'You try any more of that and I'll have you straight in gaol.'

"We have always had trouble with fan riots, even when the Stones were unknown and appearing for just a few pounds a night in the little beat clubs of West London. In fact, it was a riot that led us to being banned for the first time—from the Ricky Tick Club at Guildford. It used to meet at the Wooden Bridge pub on the Guildford by-pass, where the Stones would play on a low stage at the end of a long room with a timbered ceiling. There had been rows with the land-lord because we would never turn down our amplifiers.

This night we decided to get a better sound by slinging them from the beams. The landlord objected to this as well, and we had another row over that. Then, just by a stroke of bad luck, that very same evening a fight broke out. Like all pub fights, it grew until people were slinging punches in all directions. Naturally, he blamed us—and we were banned!

"We have been banned from many more famous places since then. One lunch time we went into the Scotch Corner pub and asked for some lunch. The manager, young and rather officious, said he would only serve us if we wore ties. 'But we never wear ties,' explained Mick. 'Those are our rules, and unless you accept them we can't serve you,' he said in a very haughty way. 'Look, if we wanted to we could buy your hotel—let alone your lunch,' said Brian as we stormed off.

"We have been banned from many other places, too—the Adelphi Hotel, Liverpool, after an all-night party; the Grand Hotel, Sheffield, after another rumpus; the Grand, Bristol, because of the way we dressed—and the Grand, Torquay, because we borrowed the lounge quartet's instruments and had an impromptu session that went on until four o'clock in the morning. The manager came down in his silk pyjamas and carpet slippers, and started to shout at us. He sacked the night porter who had opened the drink cupboard for us and then he raved at us: 'And you'll be out in the morning.' "

CHAPTER TEN

The continual disputes, controversies and occasional
court cases were good meat for Fleet Street; the
national press publicised the Rolling Stones more than
any other group during 1964-66. It made them house-
hold names, though not heroes. But on a different
level, the one that their teenage audience understood,
the Rolling Stones strode ahead, with one hit record
following another; with Mick Jagger and Keith
Richard becoming accomplished songwriters within
the limits of the group's range; with this same success
being repeated in Australia, New Zealand and Japan,
throughout Europe and Scandinavia—and especially
in the United States.

And to give them their due, the Rolling Stones
worked at an astonishing pace (as can be seen from
the chronology in the first appendix). For them, 1965
started with a short Irish tour, followed by more recording sessions, the release of their second album, and
then their first trip to Australia and New Zealand
where they toured with Roy Orbison, Rolf Harris and
Dionne Warwick. Then they appeared in Singapore,
returned to the States, made another two-week British
tour, and then spent a fortnight in Scandinavia. By
now, their riotous welcomes were no longer a local
phenomenon.

When they arrived in Sydney on January 21, a crowd
of three thousand teenagers was waiting at the airport.
About twenty of them were trampled under foot and

others were scratched and bruised when three hundred fans burst through a fence and swept through the airfield as their plane touched down. In two days, the Stones played six Sydney concerts—and were seen by twenty-seven thousand fans. At one of those shows, thirty-five fans clambered up on stage—and in Brisbane, where forty fans reached the stage, Jagger said he "almost got torn to pieces and Keith's shirt was torn so much that it looks as though he has been living in it on a desert island for two years". At Melbourne, their nine concerts there were sold out before the Rolling Stones even arrived in the city. But Andrew Oldham reported: "We've been knocked by the newspapers who keep trying to dig up scandal stories and run banner headlines about the Rolling Stones having wild all-night parties—we wish we were!"

Back in London, Mick Jagger was pulled off the stage by screaming girls on the *Ready, Steady, Go!* TV set. "I thudded down on the floor and a mass of girls smothered me. I was stamped on by scores of stiletto heels," he said. In Scandinavia, all the tickets for their concerts were sold out in two and a half hours.

Decca, realising how popular the group now was, rush-released the single *The Last Time/Play With Fire*, which they had recorded in Los Angeles en route to Australia, happily reporting in the accompanying press release:

> "*A fantastic Australian tour . . . American chart success . . . European concert triumphs. The Stones are international stars. And with this brand-new waxing they have another certain British No. 1 hit. Penned by Mick Jagger and Keith Richards,*

"The Last Time" has ringing guitar and throbbing beat behind Mick's lead vocal, with harmony on the chorus. Probably the Stones' best-ever single!

The Last Time was recorded in Hollywood en route to Australia some three weeks ago. The boys' tour there was an unqualified success, and now the all-conquering Stones are set for more trips abroad.

After a two-week theatre tour of Britain commencing at Edmonton Regal on March 5, the group flies to Scandinavia on March 24 until April 3. All seats for their concerts there were sold out within three hours.

The Stones visit Germany for three days of concerts from April 13. They then go to Paris for three days at the Olympia theatre.

A three-week American visit for TV, radio and major concert dates is also set from April 23.

The Stones hope to begin working on their first film in June. It will be a full length feature production.

PERSONAL PARS

Mick and Keith are looking for a new home. Fans have discovered their Hampstead hideaway, and the phone and doorbell never stop ringing.

Bill Wyman has an eye infection which is rather painful but not too serious.

Following the Australasian tour, Brian Jones stayed in Hollywood for a few days before coming back to London. Keith went to Paris with co-manager Andrew Oldham for a brief holiday.

Mick has had his hair cut.

1. Bill.

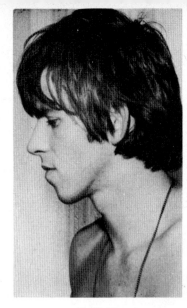

2. Keith.

3. Brian.

4. Mick.

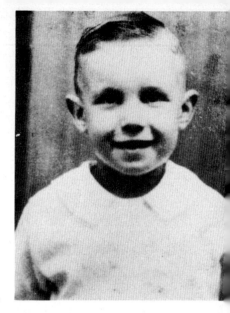

5. The young Bill Wyman.

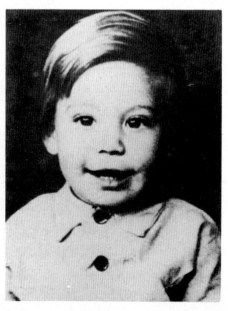

6. The young Charlie Watts

7. Mick singing.

8. Charlie Watts and his family.

9. Mick Jagger.

10. An early picture of Keith Richard.

11. Jagger as he appeared in the film *Performance*.

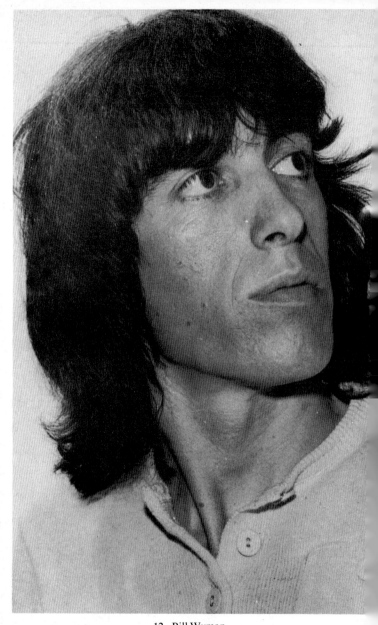

12. Bill Wyman.

13. Jagger sings.

14. Keith Richard.

15. Andrew Oldham, Stones manager (second from right) listening to play-back with Brian, Mick and engineer Glyn Johns.

16. An early TV studio shot of the Stones.

17. Brian Jones.

18. Charlie Watts.

19. Mick during the Stones tour of Europe.

20. Mick relaxes by a Viennese lake before a concert appearance in September 1973.

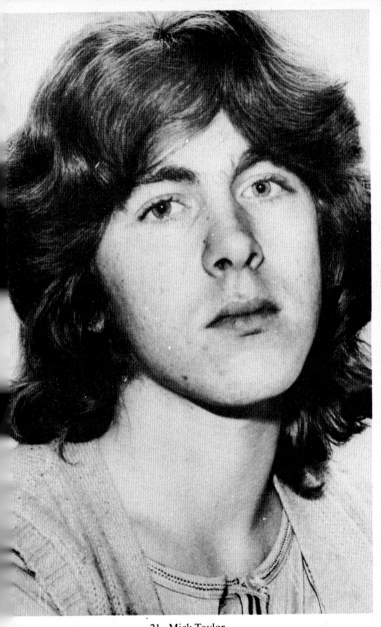

21. Mick Taylor.

22. The wedding of Mick and Bianca.

23. Billy Preston and Mick Jagger.

24. Bianca Jagger.

25. Bianca and Mick at the Blenheim Palace party.

26. Mick as he is today.

All five Stones are looking fit and bronzed after making the most of the sunshine in Australia and New Zealand."

And Andrew Loog Oldham told the *New Musical Express* that none of this success surprised him. "I'd seen it all happen before with the Beatles when I was their publicist." He agreed that the Rolling Stones were completely different. "That's why I knew they would succeed. There is always a black sheep in the pop world, someone that the Establishment can knock. In Cliff Richard's day it was Billy Fury. It's the Stones now who fill the gap."

Of course, *The Last Time* went straight to Number One—and on the very day that it did so the Stones were ordered out of another restaurant, this time the Midland Hotel, Manchester, because they were not wearing ties. By now someone was bound to complain wherever the Stones went. When they returned to the States for another tour in April, police in Georgia were swamped with complaints by passing motorists that *women* were indecently exposing themselves at a local hotel—it was only the Rolling Stones, sunbathing! At Long Beach, California, so many fans clambered on to the roof of their car that it caved in—so the group had to stand up in the car supporting the roof while their chauffeur tried to get them away with the vehicle still awash with bodies. And when they returned to the *Ed Sullivan Show* (yes, they were re-booked), the doors to the TV studios were locked for twelve hours while they recorded four numbers for the programme.

That summer they had their first Number One hit record in the States, *I Can't Get No Satisfaction*, which sold over a million copies there before it was released in this country—a number which many fans still believe is the Stones at their best.

"We cut *Satisfaction* in Los Angeles when we were working there," Mick Jagger told *Melody Maker*. "We cut quite a lot of things and that was just one—contrary to some newspaper reports it only took us just half an hour to make. We like it, but didn't think of it as a single. Then London said they had to have a single immediately because *The Last Time* was long gone and we had a "Shindig" TV date and had to have something to plug. So they just released *Satisfaction* as a single. In England, we already had the EP all pressed, the covers done and the plugs lined up before we even knew that *Satisfaction* was going to be a single . . . the Beatles had *Help* and it seemed silly to issue *Satisfaction* then. If *Help* hadn't come out then, we would have brought ours out a month ago . . . the point is that the Stones aren't in control of everything —some things are out of our hands. We make the records and have a large say in what is released in this country. But America is so different . . . I get the idea for a lyric quite separately from the songs. And Keith gets his ideas quite separately from my lyrics. Keith may play a phrase and it fits with one of my ideas for a lyric. In the case of *Satisfaction*, we thought of a phrase and the riff first and worked from there."

As one success followed another, and the Stones kept returning to the States to record, the "bad" publicity continued. Mick Jagger was said by one newspaper to have kicked a girl's bottom in the street. "She was laying into my girl and using filthy language. Sure, I kicked her," said Jagger, refuting the suggestion that he had aimed the kick because she was a Beatles fan. "She and her gang had our flat staked out for days. They were not Beatles' fans. Some papers are still trying to whip up a Stones versus Beatles war which does not exist." And Brian Jones commented: "We've always had a wild image. We built ourselves on the fact. Groups like the Hollies envy our image—I know Allan Clarke does." By now the fan scenes at their shows were often so wild that the Stones decided to give up ballroom appearances altogether because of the danger of people being injured.

The stories of riots and people being injured had now been constant for eighteen months. The "bad news" stories had been just as frequent. And in the *Daily Express*, just as the Rolling Stones had concluded a deal whereby Allen Klein became their new co-manager, Judith Simons reported: "More than a million pounds is certain to go into the bank accounts of these five young men in the next five years. Andrew Oldham, their twenty-one year old recording manager, told me: 'Under the terms of a deal concluded by our American business manager, Mr. Allen Klein, the Stones are guaranteed three million dollars over the next five years.' The deal includes renewal of their contract with Decca, who will release Stones discs in all countries except the United States and Canada . . . a year ago their fee was about £500 a show. Now they are paid £1,000 for a shorter 25-30 minute appearance. There are lucrative sidelines, too—like their spot in the American beat film *The Tami Show*. They received £25,000 for that. The Stones, ranked second to the Beatles, accept more bookings than John, George, Paul and Ringo. In the past year they have completed two tours in Britain, three in the US, two in Scandinavia, and one of Australia—approaching two hundred separate appearances. And all the time their records are bringing in the money."

She estimated that from American sales alone, they had each earned £4,000 from *Satisfaction*; that they had each earned £3,000 from *The Last Time* and also from *Little Red Rooster*, and that they had each earned another £1,500 for their earlier hits *Not Fade Away* and *It's All Over Now*. And that as songwriters Mick and Keith had each earned another £8,000.

"It isn't all profit, of course. Expenses are high. Each guitarist owns about eight instruments, and the total cost of their present equipment was £4,000. When the Stones are on tour hotel bills are about £700 a week. Salaries for secretarial and other staff accounts for £200 a week," said the *Daily Express* writer.

What she did not say, and what I know to be the case, was that all the money the Stones earned was being ploughed back fast into their business—they were hiring time in the best studios, buying the best equipment on the market, and back in 1965 they had as yet made very little. Their vast private fortunes were to come much later.

As the months rolled on, with the Stones still working at the same frantic pace they had maintained since the summer of 1963, the crowd scenes became uglier. When the group visited Dublin, the *Melody Maker* reported: "About thirty of the Irish capital's fair youths leaped the chasm of the orchestra pit on to the stage and turned a wild performance into a riot. It was a sensational close to the Rolling Stones' second concert. The youths swarmed all over the stage. Mick Jagger was dragged to the floor. Brian Jones was wrestling with three punching teenagers and Bill Wyman was forced back against a piano at the side of the stage. Keith Richard managed to escape off stage. And implacable Stone Charlie Watts carried on playing stone-faced as bedlam raged around him." At the earlier concert a bouncer punched one girl with such force that she fell to the aisle, stunned and had to be carried back to her seat by a friend. "It was wild tonight, but not as wild as when we were in Holland," said Brian Jones. Then in Belfast, fans laid seige to the group's train and the Stones had to run across tracks to cars waiting in the goods yard. At that evening's concert, the *Melody Maker* reported that fans were "jumping up and down on the seats and surging towards the stage. The seats collapsed, and an estimated seventy to eighty were smashed, with fans hurling pieces of the seats, ashtrays and bits of iron on to the stage. The injury toll was at least two serious leg injuries, innumerable fainting cases and one youth whose face was covered in blood from a head injury".

In Germany, the leading hotels in Dusseldorf refused to accommodate the group because of the risk of fan riots—and when the group arrived in the city for a press conference at the airport, thousands of fans went berserk, with two hundred of them breaking through a police cordon, attacking the police and smashing doors. In Berlin, nearly four hundred police with rubber truncheons battled with the audience after the

Stones' concert—and seventy people were injured with six policemen and thirty two fans being detained in hospital. After the show, fans pulled the emergency brake of an overhead railway train, attacked the conductor and wrecked coaches.

Only nine weeks after the release of *Satisfaction*, the Stones released *Get Off Of My Cloud/The Singer Not The Song*, and this time Decca's release said:

> "Heavy bass beat and drums lead into the latest hit number from the pens of Messrs. Jagger and Richard. The title? *Get Off Of My Cloud*—it jumped 59 places to No. 6 position in this week's US "Cash Box" Top 100 and is a certain No. 1 here.
>
> Mick handles lead vocal, and the other Stones chime in for some effective fun on the chorus. There's a big, bold beat with guitar ringing through. Very different from *Satisfaction*, the Stones' recent trans-Atlantic chart-topper and very good.
>
> Mick and Keith wrote the song during their last American trip, and the group recorded it in Hollywood. The famous five—so very different from Enid Blyton's book characters—finish their British tour this week.
>
> They fly to America for six weeks on or around October 25, to tour and play major TV shows. Before leaving they will embark on a crash programme of appearances on British television and radio for this record."

This time, the Rolling Stones reached Number One in both the British and the US charts—in the same week. And the record's success like that of *Satisfaction*, was world-wide. "It's great, marvellous," said Jagger on the phone from the States where the group was now in the middle of yet another North American tour. "We have been getting a terrific reception everywhere. Montreal and Toronto were wild. At Montreal there were so many people on stage we had to run, and then couldn't get away because there were so many people backstage. Generally, we are getting an even better reception from people than we got last time, and the American public have been less rude, too. We haven't had time to meet people as yet, but Bob Dylan visited Brian Jones at our New York hotel a couple of days ago." At that same Montreal concert, it was reported that thirty teenagers were injured and eight of them had to have hospital treatment.

On the phone to *Disc*, Mick Jagger said: "I wouldn't live in America. I don't like the country enough. I prefer England. The atmosphere is too much for me. Life is too fast here with everyone rushing around like a lot of idiots. I don't like the food because the menus lack variety. The transport cafes are better than the transport cafes in Britain but the good restaurants here are not anywhere near as good. All the food tastes pre-packed. About the only thing I like about their food is their thick ham that I have for breakfast ... you can't get Russian vodka. They won't import it and so they make their own in Florida ... they let anybody in the hotels even if they're not staying there. So that means that sometimes we get fans knocking on our door at six o'clock in the morning ... on the whole the Americans are very generous people, but they're very rude. The police are un-

103

believable. In the south they look like cowboys, wearing stetsons and carrying guns and riding motor-bikes. In towns they look like they do on the films. And they're not quietly-spoken like they are in Britain. In fact, they're loud-mouthed. In Britain I think they're a bit fed up with knocking us. But over here I don't think they'll ever reach this point. The place is so vast and it's only on this trip that we're reaching any sort of nationwide acclaim. The knockers here are madder than in Britain and more demonstrative. They're just twisted out of their minds. Because they think everything that is ever said about us is serious, lots of people think we're being hit around and are pawns in the hands of publicity men. You've only got to give a joke answer to a question and they make it into a serious statement of fact . . . we go everywhere by car. Even then in the hotel lobby the other day an eighty-year-old woman asked me if I was one of the Supremes! She wasn't kidding!"

On this trip, every concert was a sell-out, and Andrew Oldham said: "This is the boys' fourth American tour but the first one that is going to pay dividends. During this six-week period of concerts and TV appearances we will gross an unprecedented 1,500,000 dollars." On the phone again to *Disc*, Mick Jagger said from Colorado: "The whole attitude to British groups has changed. They don't like most of the groups any more. They quite like us, I think, but they have this ridiculous attitude towards us—a sort of intellectual approach towards the group." Later Charlie Watts told *Melody Maker* that some of their dates on this tour had been at universities and colleges. "At first we were amazed, because there was no screaming. They listened and then applauded at the end, just like a jazz concert. I think we'd have enjoyed this a lot more if we'd realised right away what was happening."

CHAPTER ELEVEN

By the end of that North American tour in the late autumn of 1965, the Rolling Stones seemed to realise that their career had now reached a new peak. So did Andrew Oldham who announced that the group would be on holiday for the next two months—and would not be touring Britain again for at least another six months. Like the Beatles, the group realised that when artistes reached a certain level in their careers it is time to start consolidating in a different way. For the Rolling Stones, this was the time to cement the world-wide following.

They flew to New York to appear again on the *Ed Sullivan Show*, and then began another Australasian tour, spent three weeks recording in Los Angeles, and then visited Belgium, Holland, France, Germany, Sweden and Denmark, released two more singles (*19th Nervous Breakdown* and *Paint It Black*) plus another album (*Aftermath*)—before Mick Jagger collapsed from overwork and exhaustion two weeks before they began another eight-week coast-to-coast US tour.

It was as tough a schedule as they had ever worked, but they seemed to take all this in their stride. Now, every record was an immediate Gold Disc—and of *19th Nervous Breakdown* Decca said:

"If it was possible for a disc to climb higher than No. 1, here's one that would! It's the new Rolling

Stones single, 19*th Nervous Breakdown*—this is far and away their best ever release. Watch it top the charts—not only in Britain, but all over the world.

There's a Chuck Berry-style guitar intro, setting the uptempo pace for the whole side. The Stones provide some interesting sounds here with zoom bass and fuzz-box guitar.

The lyrics by Mick Jagger and Keith Richard stand in a class of their own—lines such as 'your father's still collecting ways of making sealing wax' are typical of the Jagger-Richard's unique humorous song-writing style."

As always, the controversies followed them—just before they left for the States one of their fans committed suicide because he was told to have a hair cut; the press attacked the Stones in Australia after Brian said "Christ" in a radio interview, and Mick Jagger reported from Brisbane: "The Seekers are getting all the acclaim over here—but we're doing the business!" In Wellington, three hundred fans rioted, a policeman was taken to hospital with a fractured hand, and a girl burst an appendix. Dozens of seats at the venue, the Wellington town hall, were slashed and debris was scattered around the building. In the States, 19*th Nervous Breakdown* became their fastest-selling single.

"America is a great scene for us at present," Brian Jones told Keith Altham of the *New Musical Express*. We've never been so powerful there. I think we've reached a peak in Britain but things are still opening up for us in the States . . . there's one interesting development in the US, which does not exist for us here any more. That is, we've built up a type of intellectual following among the hippies. The Greenwich Village crowd all dig us. There was a terrible scene out there just before I left. The police were stopping and searching everybody on sight—looking for drugs, I suppose, but it was frightening. Worse than a police state."

When they toured France there were fifty-seven arrests at their Paris Olympia concert—and Bill Wyman stamped out a smoke bomb that was thrown on stage; in Marseilles, Mick Jagger received a black eye when a chair was thrown at him from the audience. "They were ripping the seats apart and beating up the gendarmes. The kids were going bonkers. Even hitting the police with their own truncheons. I kept out of it as much as possible. I don't like seeing police being thumped," said Jagger, whose eye injury required six stitches.

When their next single, *Paint It Black*, was released Decca had advance orders of two hundred thousand two weeks before the record was in the shops—and it was now eight months since the Rolling Stones had last made a British TV appearance. Now they were thinking of producing their own promotional films to plug new records. In subtle ways like this which gave them more control over their work was the emphasis of their career changing. When the single came out, Decca stated:

"It goes without saying that the disc will hit the chart-tops in no time flat. *Paint It Black* was written by Mick Jagger and Keith Richard during the

Stones' Australian tour last March. The boys recorded it in Hollywood after the tour. 'They've recorded everything in America for about eighteen months now,' says manager Andrew Oldham, 'except *As Tears Go By*. We made that in England because we wanted the special string quartet sound.'

Paint It Black features Brian Jones working very hard on sitar, giving the disc an Indian sound. Charlie Watts doubles on drums and electric castanets.

A Moat for Keith

"Stone Keith has recently bought a house in Sussex. 'It's gorgeous,' he says, 'and has a moat around it.'

He's the third member of the group to emigrate from London to Sussex—Bill and Charlie bought houses there last year.

Brian and Mick still live in London flats. Mick's latest possession is a week-old dark blue Aston Martin sports car. 'My pride and joy,' he says."

By the week of its release, the single had sold four hundred thousand copies. And the *Daily Express* chose the occasion to say: "Now at this moment of conventional success, their singer 22 year old Mick Jagger has revealed himself in his true light . . . not rude, not rebellious, not arrogant. He said yesterday: 'When I was sixteen I wanted to be a journalist. But it seemed too much like hard work. When I went to university (the London School of Economics) to study politics and economics I thought of going into politics. But I believe it is harder initially to get into politics and then get to the top than it is in the pop world. There are parallels one can draw between the two fields. In selling yourself as a politician, like selling records, not so much depends on what you have to say but on how you say it. The last election has proved the selling power of an image on television.' "

This was the year that the Rolling Stones peaked throughout the world. And they knew it. And so did Andrew Oldham. Now, they started speaking less frequently to the press. The public outrages became fewer. Long periods elapsed between their records. But they still worked extraordinarily hard, still accepting far more bookings—mostly overseas—than the Beatles.

But success brought even more problems; when they made their next US tour fourteen of the top hotels in New York all refused to accommodate the group for fear of the destruction so often caused by their fans, and it was an understandable reaction. When they arrived in the city, police had to use tear gas and truncheons to disperse the fans—and Oldham hired a sailing yacht, the SS Sea Panther, so the group could be less accessible. But, as on their previous trip, the Stones were now aware that they were receiving a different reaction from the actual audiences—and even from the press who had been hostile in the past.

Phoning the *New Musical Express* from Missouri in the middle of the tour, Mick Jagger said: "One thing I will say about the American Press this time is that in spite of the rubbish written by the usual idiots who come back to the dressing room and say, 'Which one of you is Ringo?', we are getting great reviews. Even the reporters who have written more personal articles have given the concerts rave write-ups. In Chicago—

which is a great place for people chucking chair-legs at you—and in St. Louis we got tremendous receptions. In Houston we got ten thousand turn up to see us, which is very big for Houston. Boston was an unbelievable scene. We played in a baseball park and the police used tear gas after the performance to disperse the crowd who had invaded the square."

In Montreal, the Stones stopped one concert to boo the bouncers hired to guard them. Later, Mick told *Disc*: "It was unbelievable. We've never seen anything like it before. I was disgusted. There were about thirty bouncers when we appeared—all of them huge blokes, wrestlers, I think. They were punching people up for no reason at all and then throwing them out. One fight broke out at the front of the theatre while we were playing and six of the chaps set on one kid. It was terrible. It was going on in front of twelve thousand people, too. In the end we stopped playing because the fans were booing and hissing and pointing at the bouncers. We joined in—and after the show had to run for our lives because the wrestlers tried to get up on the stage after us. I was scared out of my life. I thought we were going to get it that time."

Back in Britain, public appearances by the Stones were becoming rarer and rarer; their only stage performance in nearly a year had been at the annual *New Musical Express* Poll Winners' concert, and then they had refused to allow the show to be filmed. So when the group appeared at the Royal Albert Hall on September 23rd before a crowd of five thousand it now became a major occasion within the music business and Decca presented them with *twenty* Gold Discs to mark the fact that each of their last four US albums had grossed more than one million US dollars. Their performance was recorded live, and afterwards the Stones hosted a party which was filmed for the BBC TV programme *Top Of The Pops*.

There was no doubt now that the Rolling Stones had become highly exclusive. In the *New Musical Express*, Norrie Drummond reported that: "It was the pop world's social event of the year—the opening night last Friday at London's Albert Hall of the Rolling Stones tour, 1966. John Entwistle and Keith Moon of the Who, Jonathan King and ex-Yardbird Paul Samwell-Smith were among the names in the audience. Guests at a private party after the show included John Maus and Gary Leeds, Chris Curtis, who arrived with RSG's Vicki Wickham, Lionel Bart, deejay Alan Freeman and Cathy McGowan. Brian Jones told me at the party that he had felt decidedly nervous when fans stormed the stage. And he had every reason to be. As soon as the group appeared on stage hundreds of screaming teenagers surged to the front of the stage, elbowed their way past the security men and climbed on to the platform. Keith Richard was knocked to the ground. Mick was almost strangled, while Brian Jones and Bill Wyman took to their heels, followed closely by dozens of determined fans. Charlie Watts sat quietly behind his drums, watching the scene.

"Manager Andrew Oldham rushed on stage, followed by the group's agent Tito Burns and their publicist Les Perrin, to help the bouncers. Even Troggs manager Larry Page and deejay Chris Denning, who were sitting near me in the front row, ran forward to help. The group disappeared and it was announced that unless everyone returned to their seats the show would be cancelled. The stage was cleared. Fans drifted back to their seats and the Stones reappeared.

"Mick—dressed in orange shirt, white bell-bottomed trousers and black, sequined, Chinese-style jacket—ran forward and started with *Paint It Black*. Then came *Under My Thumb* and *Get Off Of My Cloud*. Charlie then walked to the front of the stage and announced *Lady Jane* and returned to his drumkit. For *Lady Jane*, Brian, looking elegant in grey trousers, purple velvet jacket, red silk shirt and white cravat, sat down to play an instrument resembling an electric zither. *Not Fade Away*, *The Last Time*, *Have You Seen Your Mother, Baby, Standing In The Shadow* followed before they closed with *Satisfaction*."

The penultimate song, *Have You Seen Your Mother, Baby, Standing In The Shadow*, was their latest single; to promote it, they dressed in women's clothing and wore make-up. "We did it for a laugh. I thought it was all a bit of a giggle, really," said Jagger, though one could not help feeling that this was now sensation for sensation's sake—a feeling that persisted when they chose to appear on *Sunday Night At The London Palladium* to promote their next single, *Let's Spend The Night Together*, and then refused to take part in what was the traditional (though admittedly rather boring) finale to the show, the round-about. "The only reason we did the show was because it was a good national plug—anyone who thought we were changing our image to suit a family audience was mistaken," Mick Jagger told the *New Musical Express*. The show was the top programme in that week's TV ratings, viewed in 9,250,000 homes—but Jagger afterwards told the *Daily Express*: "It was a mediocre show, and it made us the same. It was all terrible. I'm not saying we were any better than the other acts—it was just too depressing. We were dreading the Palladium performance and we will never do a programme there again. Added to that, television sound is pretty poor and does not match our sound on records."

To which the obvious answer was: Why did they agree to do the show in the first place if they felt so strongly?

By now, months often passed without the Rolling Stones appearing in public—and when they did so, it was usually either on the Continent or across the Atlantic. In Britain, they were living more private lives —until suddenly in February, 1967, came the event that emphasised even further the distance that had developed between the Rolling Stones and their traditional teenage audience. And that was the first drug raid.

There were already signs that the awe with which they were now being treated by fans in the United States was something that the Rolling Stones were beginning to take very seriously. In an interview with Keith Altham of the *New Musical Express*, Brian Jones said: "Our generation is growing up with us and they believe in the same things we do . . . our real followers have moved on with us—some of those we like most are the hippies in New York, but nearly all of them think like us and are questioning some of the basic immoralities which are tolerated in present day society —the war in Vietnam, persecution of homosexuals, illegality of abortion, drug taking. All these things are immoral. We are making our own statement—others are making more intellectual ones. Our friends are

114

questioning the wisdom of an almost blind acceptance of religion compared with total disregard for reports related to things like unidentified flying objects which seems more real to me. Conversely I don't underestimate the power or influence of those, unlike me, who do believe in God. We believe there can be no evolution without revolution. I realise there are other inequalities—the ratio between affluence and reward for work done is all wrong. I know I earn too much but I'm still young and there's something spiteful inside me which makes me want to hold on to what I've got. I believe we are moving toward a new age in ideas and events. Astrologically we are at the end of the age called Pisces—at the beginning of which people like Christ were born. We are soon to begin the age of Aquarius, in which events as important as those at the beginning of Pisces are likely to occur."

After that controversial Palladium appearance, which inspired an avalanche of letters to the press (thirty-to-one against the Stones according to the *Daily Mirror*), Jagger appeared alone on the Eamonn Andrews TV chat show, talking intelligently and perceptively, and eclipsing two lesser show business figures who attacked him, singer Susan Maughan and comedian Terry Scott. "They weren't big showbiz names," he said waspishly to *Melody Maker* afterwards. "C'mon—Susan Maughan. Who's she? She's had about one hit record in five years. She's kept up by an occasional picture in the *Daily Sketch*. As for Terry Scott—when I was very small and had an infantile sense of humour, he used to amuse me. I couldn't believe that he really has the mentality that he portrays when he does those schoolboy things. But he really *has* got a schoolboy mentality. All those people have got is a non-existent glitter which they believe surrounds them and separates them from the rest of the world. I'm sure Susan Maughan thinks she's surrounded by this terrific glow. She acts like it. She has a poodle and the whole scene. The poodle's called Bobby's Girl after the hit record she made. Big showbiz names don't act like that at all. They accept people on their own terms."

Then came the first of the drug-taking allegations in the *News of the World*, which was followed within a few days by a drugs raid on Keith Richard's country home in Sussex where Mick Jagger and his new girl-friend Marianne Faithfull were spending the weekend with Keith and other friends (Mick's three year romance with Chrissie Shrimpton had now ended). Jagger's mother, Mrs. Eva Jagger, was interviewed by *The Sunday Express* and said: "I don't think Mike takes drugs. But if they have been having a lark they will have to take the consequences." And of Marianne, she said: "Well, I won't say I wouldn't prefer her to be single. But really Mike's generation has different standards about this sort of thing. I think they possibly came together because they are both a bit lonely. She is estranged from her husband and Mike, despite all his fame, has a rather lonely existence. Remember it's not very easy for him to meet girls as other boys do . . . I don't think Mike is rebelling against us. In fact, I'm not sure he is rebelling against anything. He often has his tongue in his cheek, you know. Although we don't see very much of him now, we are still a very close family. Mike has always said it would embarrass both him and us if, like some pop stars, he bought us a new home. It's true, we would be embarrassed.

But he is very kind with presents and he would give us anything we needed . . . he is very considerate. If he knows there is going to be something sensational about him in the newspapers he always phones to warn us and tell us not to worry. It infuriates me to know that some people regard him as a moron. He is a very intelligent, sensitive boy . . . I just wish he would stay out of trouble."

But by this time, Mick and Keith were in big trouble. Although they kept on working, and made another triumphant European tour, and Mick and Marianne were now looking for a country estate, the police were busily preparing charges against the two Stones after that drugs raid. Keith was eventually accused of allowing the premises to be used for smoking Indian hemp, and Mick was charged with being in unlawful possession of amphetamine tablets.

Before the case came to Court, the Rolling Stones completed that European tour (including concerts in Eastern Europe), which was accompanied by the usual scenes of violence, and Jagger was interviewed by *Melody Maker* in his Paris hotel suite. He told the paper: "Since the peak of the Beatles and Stones there have been a lot of big groups but none with any real flair—except for the Who and the Jimi Hendrix Experience. I have got some ideas on how to change things—to do something different, but I don't want to say what they are, and I'm not even sure that I want to do them. It would be very expensive—and then it's so difficult to tell whether it would be a success. For example, on this tour we played in Rome and all the people in the front rows were over twenty-five—a lot of them over forty. They were all socialites—so we had to give a proper concert and play really well. This is just what we wanted to do at the Albert Hall—but the kids didn't want it . . . people talk about the riots that happen when we play. Of course there is a certain violent element, and, to a certain extent, the kids are conforming to what is expected of them. But there is more to it than that . . . I've seen this wild behaviour in so many countries and the pattern is always the same. Because it is the same symptom. Frustration. And these are kids from all kinds of environments . . . you can't solve the problem by locking them up . . . that isn't the answer—you have to find out why it is that kids are discontented. They are not all morons just spoiling for a fight with the police."

And of the police themselves, Jagger said: "Everyone knows that Britain is short of police—but they send big groups of them raiding clubs and even barns in Lincolnshire. It's madness. The situation is not only becoming ridiculous, but frightening. You sit at home and you think you are safe because you are not in South Africa or some other police state. But when suddenly the police move in it's very disturbing and you begin to wonder just how much freedom you really have . . . there are only about a thousand real addicts in Britain and nobody is going to make a fortune peddling heroin because the addicts can get it on prescription. But if you stop this, the Mafia will move in and we're going to have the same problem as America."

And to the *Daily Mirror* when he returned from the tour, Jagger said: "I see a great deal of danger in the air . . . teenagers are not screaming over pop music any more, they're screaming for much deeper reasons. We are only serving as a means of giving them an outlet. Pop music is just the superficial tissue to it all . . . when I'm on stage, I sense that the teenagers are trying to communicate to me, like by telepathy, a message of some urgency. Not about me or about our music, but about the world and the way we live . . . teenagers the world over are weary of being pushed around by half-witted politicians who attempt to dominate their way of thinking and set a code for their living. They want to be free and have the right of expression; of thinking and living aloud without any petty restrictions. This doesn't mean they want to become alcoholics or drug-takers or tread down on their parents. This is a protest against the system. I see a lot of trouble coming in the dawn."

Jagger was right. Trouble was coming—and not just for him and Keith Richard. On May 10th, it was Brian Jones' turn to be arrested at his London flat and to be charged with unlawful possession of cannabis. And that same day the magistrates' court hearing opened in the Jagger-Richard case. They both reserved their defence and pleaded not guilty, and with their friend art gallery director Robert Fraser they were sent for trial on bail of £100.

By now, it is fairly clear from the interviews from which I have quoted that at least some of the Stones regarded themselves as symbols of a movement, a trend in opinion and in philosophy, that went far beyond their music. At this crucial moment, all the forces of the law combined to act with a collective stupidity that seemed to underline the validity of everything the Stones had said.

The Jagger-Richard trial opened at the West Sussex Quarter Sessions before Judge Block on June 27th.

Fraser pleaded guilty to a charge of being in unlawful possession of twenty-four tablets of heroin on the night of the raid, and then the case opened against the other two, with Jagger's private doctor telling the Court that the pills he had had were of a kind widely used by "people with a busy day ahead of them", and that though Mick had bought them in Italy (where they were available without a prescription) he had told him (the doctor) about them, and that he (the doctor) had said they were all right to use in an emergency but on no account must he take them regularly. The Judge then told the jury: "I have ruled in law that these remarks cannot be regarded as a prescription by a duly authorised medical practitioner and it therefore follows that the defence open to Mr. Jagger is not available to him. I therefore direct you that there is no defence to this charge." After an absence of five minutes, the jury found Mick Jagger guilty and he was taken to the remand wing of Lewes prison. The following day, Keith Richard's case was heard—and he, too, was found guilty.

By now, Jagger was being photographed in police handcuffs—and so was Richard. And when the time came to pass sentence, Keith Richard was told he would be sent to gaol for twelve months with £500 costs; Robert Fraser to gaol for six months with £200 costs, and Mick Jagger to gaol for three months with £100 costs. That night Mick Jagger was taken to Brixton Prison and Keith Richard and Robert Fraser to Wormwood Scrubs. There was an immediate press outcry at these astonishing sentences, at the handcuffing—and within twenty four hours Mick and Keith were both released on £17,000 bail. In *The Times*, the editor himself Mr. William Rees-Mogg, wrote the now-famous editorial:—

WHO BREAKS A BUTTERFLY ON A WHEEL?

"Mr. Jagger has been sentenced to imprisonment for three months. He is appealing against conviction and sentence, and has been granted bail until the hearing of the appeal later in the year. In the meantime, the sentence of imprisonment is bound to be widely discussed by the public. And the circumstances are sufficiently unusual to warrant some discussion in the public interest.

"Mr. Jagger was charged with being in possession of four tablets containing amphetamine sulphate and methyl amphetamine hydrochloride; these tablets had been bought, perfectly legally, in Italy and brought back to this country. They are not a highly dangerous drug, or in proper dosage a dangerous drug at all. They are of the benzedrine type and the Italian manufacturers recommend them as both a stimulant and as a remedy for travel sickness.

"In Britain it is an offence to possess these drugs without a doctor's prescription. Mr. Jagger's doctor says that he knew and had authorised their use, but he did not give a prescription for them as indeed they had already been purchased. His evidence was not challenged. This was therefore an offence of a technical character, which before this case drew the point to public attention any honest man might have been liable to commit.

"If after his visit to the Pope, the Archbishop of Canterbury had bought proprietory airsickness pills on Rome airport, and imported the unused tablets on his return, he would have risked committing precisely the same offence. No one who has ever travelled and bought proprietory drugs abroad can be sure that he has not broken the law. "Judge Block directed the jury that the approval of a doctor was not a defence in law to the charge of possessing drugs without a prescription, and the jury convicted. Mr. Jagger was not charged with complicity in any other drug offence that occurred in the same house.

"They were separate cases, and no evidence was produced to suggest that he knew that Mr. Fraser had heroin tablets or that the vanishing Mr. Sneidermann had cannabis resin. It is indeed no offence to be in the same building or the same company as people possessing or even using drugs, nor could it reasonbaly be made an offence.

"The drugs which Mr. Jagger had in his possession must therefore be treated on their own, as a separate issue from the other drugs that other people may have had in their possession at the same time. It may be difficult for lay opinion to make this distinction clearly, but obviously justice cannot be done if one man is to be punished for a purely contingent association with someone else's offence.

"We have, therefore, a conviction against Mr. Jagger purely on the ground that he possessed four Italian pep pills, quite legally bought though not legally imported without a prescription. Four is not a large number. This is not the quantity which a pusher of drugs would have on him, nor even the quantity one would expect in an addict.

"In any case, Mr. Jagger's career is obviously one that does involve great personal strain and exhaustion; his doctor says that he approved the occasional use of these drugs, and it seems likely that similar drugs would have been prescribed if there was a need for them. Millions of similar drugs are prescribed in Britain every year, and for a variety of conditions.

"One has to ask, therefore, how it is that this technical offence, divorced as it must be from other people's offences, was thought to deserve the penalty of imprisonment. In the courts at large it is most uncommon for imprisonment to be imposed on first offenders where the drugs are not major drugs of addiction and there is no question of drug traffic.

"The normal penalty is probation, and the purpose of probation is to encourage the offender to develop his career and to avoid the drug risks in the future. It is surprising therefore that Judge Block should have decided to sentence Mr. Jagger to imprisonment, and particularly surprising as Mr. Jagger's is about as mild a drug case as can ever have been brought before the Courts.

"It would be wrong to speculate on the Judge's reasons, which we do not know. It is, however, possible to consider the public reaction. There are many people who take a primitive view of the matter, what one might call a pre-legal view of the matter. They consider that Mr. Jagger has 'got what was coming to him'. They resent the anarchic quality of the Rolling Stones' performance, dislike their songs, dislike their influence on teenagers and broadly suspect them of decadence, a word used by Miss Monica Furlong in the *Daily Mail*.

"As a sociological concern this may be reasonable enough, and at an emotional level it is very understandable, but it has nothing to do with the case. One has to ask a different question: has Mr. Jagger received the same treatment as he would have received if he had not been a famous figure, with all the criticism and resentment his celebrity has aroused? If a promising undergraduate had come back from a summer visit to Italy with four pep pills in his pocket would it have been thought right to ruin his career by sending him to prison for three months? Would it also have been thought necessary to display him handcuffed to the public?

"There are cases in which a single figure becomes the focus for public concern about some aspect of public morality. The Stephen Ward case, with its dubious evidence and questionable verdict, was one of them, and that verdict killed Stephen Ward. There are elements of the same emotion in the reactions to this case.

"If we are going to make any case a symbol of the conflict between the sound traditional values of Britain and the new hedonism, then we must be sure that the sound traditional values include those of tolerance and equity.

"It should be the particular quality of British justice to ensure that Mr. Jagger is treated exactly the same as anyone else, no better and no worse.

"There must remain a suspicion in this case that Mr. Jagger received a more severe sentence than would have been thought proper for any purely anonymous young man."

Other national newspaper writers also came to Mick Jagger's defence. Rudolf Klein and Eric Clark said in *The Observer* that sending the two Stones to prison "is almost certain to have precisely the opposite effect from the one intended. Far from discouraging others, the case has produced two martyrs . . . the judge's sentences must have seemed like the verdict of one generation on another". In an editorial, *The Guardian* said that "if the Chichester case, with its excessive accompaniments of adulation and handcuffing, reduces the public discussion over drugs to the level of Swingers versus Squares this will be a memorial to the maladroitness of the authorities, but also a sizeable tragedy".

The controversy raged in the letter columns of the press. Many other papers published editorials on the issue. The role of the *News of the World*, who passed the original information about the party at Richard's house to the Police, came under fire in other papers and amongst politicians.

And, much more quickly than had originally been expected, a date was set for the appeals to be heard in the High Court by the Lord Chief Justice himself, Lord Parker, and Lord Justice Winn and Mr. Justice Cusack. Lord Parker made it quite clear that they were unanimous in thinking that the evidence that a girl at the party had been sitting in the room naked with a fur rug or bedspread over her shoulders "was extremely prejudicial", and should not have been introduced into Richard's case. And the case against him and the verdict was quashed. In Jagger's case, Lord Parker said: "There were only four tablets left in the phial, there was no evidence of over-indulgence, peddling to others, and they were amphetamine drugs. In no sense were they, as the Court had recently to deal with, heroin. Further, the evidence of the doctor was the strongest mitigation there could be. Granted it was not a prescription, it was something the appellant was taking with the full knowledge of the doctor. The proper course was to give a conditional discharge ... I think it is right to say that when one is dealing with somebody who has great responsibilities as you have— because you are, whether you like it or not, an idol of a large number of the young in this country—being in that position you have very grave responsibilities, and if you do come to be punished it is only natural that those responsibilities should carry a higher penalty." At a subsequent press conference, Mick Jagger said: "One doesn't ask for responsibilities; they have been thrust upon one. I simply ask for my private life to be left alone. My responsibility is only to myself."

Once the case was over, the Rolling Stones returned to their more usual arena; their next release *We Love You/Dandelion* even featured clanking cell doors as the introduction to the A-side, which I felt at the time (and so did many critics) was one of the worst records they had ever made—it only reached Number Eight in the British hit parade, whereas nearly all their other recent singles had gone to Number One. Both in its form and in its lyrics, the song seemed much inferior to the Beatles' *All You Need Is Love*, which had the same contemporary message. Indeed, although the Rolling Stones had now reached a level of symbolism, a style of chic mystique, musically I felt something was lacking—something that in my view they have never fully regained. Their next album *Their Satanic Majesties Request* also seemed to me to be poorer in quality—though it still grossed two million dollars in its first ten days of release in the US.

As Gomelski commented to me, the Rolling Stones now seemed to be more concerned with their image than their music. That may be unfair to them; but that was the way it seemed.

CHAPTER TWELVE

The image that the Rolling Stones now had, and Mick
Jagger in particular, was one that was no longer dir-
ectly based on their career as musicians. It was a change
of emphasis and one that has remained to this day.
After the success of the appeal by Mick Jagger and
Keith Richard to the High Court, press and television
elevated the group to a new level in the media mind
beyond that of mere entertainers—one in which it did
not seem incongruous to fly Mick Jagger by helicopter
to Spain's Hall near Ongar, Essex, the home of Sir
John Ruggles-Brise, so that he could be interviewed
in a sedate country home atmosphere for ITV's *World
In Action*. There, waiting for him in the garden with
almost apostolic respect were Mr. William Rees-Mogg,
whose editorial in *The Times* had done so much to
influence public opinion; Lord Stow Hill, himself formerly one of the chief law officers of the Crown as
Sir Frank Soskice; the Bishop of Woolwich and the
Jesuit priest, Father Corbishley. There they all discussed the significance of the case with due solemnity
and, as the reviewer in *The Times* put it, "whether or
not society was corrupt and the extent to which absol-
ute freedom was desirable".

It was the beginning of an entirely new era in pop
music. It ceased to be called that for a start; it was
now "rock music". It was an art form. It was treated
with gravity by the Sunday papers. To analyse a song's

lyrics became all important. And the artistes themselves started becoming very aware of their status in the social firmament.

The Rolling Stones' own image started to take a strange shape when Brian Jones became the next member of the group to be sent to gaol and then have the sentence set aside; as his health which had often been suspect worsened and he needed regular medical treatment; as the group established their own offices in London; as they parted company with Andrew Oldham who had for so long been their mentor and attempted to produce their own recording sessions—until the penny dropped and they had the sense to bring in the brilliant American producer Jimmy Miller to work with them on their future records; as Brian Jones brought them back into the drugs controversy when he was arrested yet again on another charge.

Two years passed without the Rolling Stones making any British public appearances, though with Miller as their producer they regained some of their old flair with singles like *Jumping Jack Flash* and *Honky Tonk Women*. But these were issued fourteen months apart —and there was a major dispute between the group and Decca over the cover of their *Beggar's Banquet* album.

By now they were becoming exclusive in all areas of their lives, limiting their personal appearances, releasing records much less frequently, speaking to the press much more rarely, seldom appearing on television, and organising their private lives in a style that befitted their status with Jagger buying a large country estate and a London town house in Cheyne Walk, with Watts buying the country home of Lord Shawcross, and Jones moving into the former Sussex home of A. A. Milne, author of *Winnie the Pooh*.

Now, more than ever, Mick Jagger was *The* Rolling Stone as far as the media were concerned, an international celebrity in his own right, publicised whatever he did. Without the group he moved into films with starring appearances in *Performance* and *Ned Kelly*. The next time he appeared in court on a drugs charge, the case received little publicity compared with the previous one and he was merely fined.

Internally, the group had problems—and Brian Jones eventually left the Rolling Stones in June, 1969, saying: "I no longer see eye to eye with the others over the discs we are cutting." He was replaced by Mick Taylor, who made his debut on the *Honky Tonk Women* single. And within a month Brian Jones was dead—found drowned in the swimming pool at his home.

Taylor was first seen in public at the free concert in Hyde Park, when two hundred and fifty thousand fans saw butterflies released in the air in Brian's memory and heard Mick Jagger read an exerpt from Shelley in his memory as he stood on stage, dressed in a white frock. The single was an immediate Number One hit, and Taylor told *Disc*: "Of course, it's nice and exciting, but I knew it would happen. It doesn't really surprise me. After all, you don't join a group like the Stones and expect failure do you? People don't actually attack me in the street, but when I go to clubs now it's a strange feeling. I can sense people staring at me. Once nobody knew me from the next bloke. Now, they obviously recognise me and it's a weird feeling. I feel very much part of the group now—and much more comfortable." Taylor, who had previously worked with John

Mayall, said: "I was a bit nervous when I went to the Stones' session—obviously—I hadn't met them or even seen them play before. But after a couple of minutes I felt really comfortable and at ease. After all with Mayall I'd been playing blues, the Stones play heavy rock and really there's not that much difference."

During October, November and December, Taylor made his first US tour with the Rolling Stones, and at Altamont a member of the audience trying to get to the stage was stabbed to death by Hells Angels; the *Let It Bleed* and *Get Your Ya Yas Out!* albums became the Rolling Stones' last LPs for Decca; the group broke with Allen Klein; Jagger's two films were released; their 1970 European tour was as sensational as any they had ever made with arrests, fights and even tear gas in Milan—but the Stones spent most of that year relaxing at their country homes or on holiday abroad; as 1971 dawned, it became apparent that they would not re-sign with Decca now that their contract had expired—and in March it was announced that the group would be leaving England to live in France. By now, Mick Jagger's romance with Marianne Faithfull was over; Bill Wyman's divorce was behind him; Keith Richard and Anita Pallenberg had a family of their own; Mick Taylor had a life of almost total anonymity when not working, and Charlie and Shirley had a daughter and a life of serenity. The Stones made a farewell British tour, and the *Daily Telegraph* reported that the group had grossed an estimated £83,000,000 so far during their career. The paper reported on their decision to live in the South of France: "The move was announced yesterday in Newcastle, where the group appeared in two concerts at the start of its first British tour for more than four years. It will be a farewell tour. A spokesman said the group had had 'long and complicated' talks with lawyers and financial advisers. Tax experts said yesterday that the Stones could gain personal taxation advantages by becoming French residents. Income-tax in France is generally lower than in this country. On royalties from records played in Britain, they would pay only the difference between their tax rate in Britain and their rate in France. This might only be a couple of shillings in the pound. Mr. Leslie Perrin, the spokesman, said that the move was 'not a case of running away from the taxman'. The main reason was that the Stones liked France tremendously . . . (the Stones) will retain their British citizenship and record in this country. Mr. Perrin said: 'They are taking homes in France. But they are not turning their backs on Britain, which they like very much.' "

Soon after they arrived in France, the *New Musical Express reported*: "It was officially announced last weekend that the Rolling Stones have signed with the Kinney Group—as was widely expected—and that their recordings will henceforth be released world-wide on a newly-created label called Rolling Stones Records. The group's first album under the new deal will be released next Friday (April 23), comprising ten Jagger-Richard compositions—they are *Brown Sugar*, *Sway*, *Wild Horses*, *Can't You Hear Me Knocking*, *You Gotta Move*, *Bitch*, *I Got The Blues*, *Sister Morphine*, *Dead Flowers* and *Moonlight Mile*. Titled *Sticky Fingers*, it was produced by Jimmy Miller, and will be issued in a special cover designed by Andy Warhol. Meanwhile the Stones' first single on their new label is rushed out today. The Kinney Group is a relatively new organisation including the Warner Brothers, Reprise, and Elektra labels. Atlantic is also part of the Kinney set-up in America, where the Rolling Stones label will be distributed through Atlantic's Atco subsidiary—and it was Atlantic chief Ahmet Ertegun who tied up the deal . . . the contract initially covers a four-year period, during which time the Stones guarantee to produce six albums including *Sticky Fingers*. But there is also the possibility that, in addition to these six group albums, there may be some solo LPs projecting various members of the Stones individually."

What lay behind all this was money. Big money. The details have never been divulged. The information I have is only second-hand and so cannot be repeated—but it is no secret that this deal made the Rolling Stones one of the wealthiest groups in the history of pop music. It gave them total financial independence. It cemented their social position.

Soon after this Mick Jagger announced that he was to marry Bianca Perez Morena de Macias, former girlfriend of actor Michael Caine—and Mick hired a private jet to fly a planeload of guests including Paul McCartney and Ringo Starr, several Faces, and various aristocrats and his own family to St. Tropez for the wedding. In October, their daughter Jade was born—and in 1972 and 1973, the Rolling Stones were back working just as hard as ever, but this time to some of the largest audiences in the world, grossing phenomenal record sales, and now indisputably a sociological phenomenon as well. Now, Jagger could raise £200,000 from one concert to help the earthquake victims of Managua, Nicaragua, his wife's home town. They could draw an audience of thirty thousand in New Zealand—or forty-eight thousand in Washington. Their first European tour in three years was described by Bill Wyman as "the best tour we've ever done, really. You've got the craziness still, but, everything is so much better organised than it was two or three years ago. The more you're in control, the better it all is".

APPENDIX 1

ROLLING STONES CHRONOLOGY

Where were you in '62? So ran the recent nostalgic advertising campaign for the rock film *American Graffiti*. In 1962, Mick Jagger, Keith Richard and Brian Jones were sharing a small flat in Edith Grove, Fulham. They had come together after Brian had advertised in *Jazz News* for musicians wanting to form a rhythm 'n' blues group. At first, they called themselves The Rollin' Stones (without the 'G'), and appeared for as little as £5 a night in the West London clubs. On Boxing Day, 1962, they appeared at the Piccadilly Club, London, and then early in the new year came the residency at the Crawdaddy Club which met at the Station Hotel, Richmond. Their first major press story appeared in *The Richmond and Twickenham Times* on April 13th., and it was with that cutting that George Tremlett started his Rolling Stones files on which this chronology – the most detailed so far published on the group – is based:

1963

January		Charlie Watts joins the group.
February		First recording session at the IBC studios in Portland Place, London. Begin eight-month residency at the Crawdaddy – Station Hotel, Richmond.
April	13	First press story appears in the *Richmond and Twickenham Times*.
April	21	Beatles go down to Richmond to see the Stones. Go back afterwards to the Edith Grove flat, and subsequently recommend the group to their ex-publicist Andrew Oldham.

135

April	28	Andrew Oldham and Eric Easton go down to Richmond to see the Stones for the first time at the Crawdaddy.
May	3	Andrew Oldham and Eric Easton sign the Rolling Stones to management contract after buying their IBC tapes for £90.
May	10	Rolling Stones record their first single *Come On/I Wanna Be Loved* at Olympic Studios with Oldham as producer.
June	7	*Come On/I Wanna Be Loved* released by Decca. Group make their TV debut on *Thank Your Lucky Stars*.
June	13	First national press mention. Daily Mirror feature reports that the Stones have a new dance "which you will see nowhere in the world but Richmond ... or maybe you just like to listen to the music which is very exciting anyway".
August	2	Feature in the *New Musical Express* says: "The Rolling Stones first burst into prominence as the long haired London group with a twitch that was a kind of dance ..."
August	5	Botwell House, Hayes.
August	6	Thames Hotel, Windsor.
August	9	California ballroom, Dunstable.
August	10	Handsworth Plaza doubling with Oldhill Plaza, Birmingham.
August	30	Tower Ballroom, New Brighton.
September	29	Stones begin their first major British tour with Bo Diddley and the Everly Brothers at the New Victoria, London.
November	1	*I Wanna Be Your Man* (written by John Lennon and Paul McCartney)/*Stoned* released by Decca.

November	28	Gene Pitney meets them and is quoted in the *Daily Mirror*: "When I first saw them I didn't know whether to say hello or bark. But then I got to know them. They're something; really something."

1964

January		First EP released – *Poison Ivy/Money/You'd Better Move On/Bye Bye Johnny*.
January	6	Stones begin their first bill-topping tour at the Harrow Granada supported by the Ronettes and Marty Wilde.
January	8	Mansfield.
January	9	Kettering.
January	10	Walthamstow.
January	12	Tooting.
January	14	Maidstone.
January	15	Bedford.
January	18	Woolwich.
January	19	Coventry Theatre.
January	26	Leicester de Montford.
February	8	Package tour with John Leyton opens at Edmonton, London. Described as "caveman-like quintet" in subsequent review in *New Musical Express*.
February	14	*Not Fade Away/Little By Little* released by Decca. The A-side was originally written and recorded by Buddy Holly and the Crickets. The B-side was co-written by Mick Jagger and Phil Spector who plays maraccas on the track.
April	17	First album *The Rolling Stones* released. Tracks: *Route 66/I Just Wanna Make Love To You/Honest I Do/I Need You Baby/Now I've Got A Witness Like Uncle Phil and Uncle Gene/Little By*

137

*Little/I'm A King Bee/Carol/Tell Me
(You're Coming Back)/Can I Get A
Witness/You Can Make It If You Try/
Walking The Dog.*

April	18	Mad Mod Ball at Wembley. Thirty arrests.
April	20–21	International TV Festival in Montreux.
April	22	Daily Mirror reports: "Mr. Wallace Scowcroft, President of the National Federation of Hairdressers, offered a free haircut to the next number one group or soloist in the pop chart, adding: 'The Rolling Stones are the worst. One of them looks as if he has got a feather duster on his head.'"
April	26	*New Musical Express* Poll Winners' concert at Wembley.
May	1	Jack Hutton reports in the *Daily Mirror* on the Stones: "As if by a pre-arranged signal, all five simultaneously pulled down the skin under their eyes and pushed up their noses. Believe me it's frightening . . ."
May	9	Savoy Rooms, Catford.
May	10	Colston Hall, Bristol.
May	10	Disc jockey Jimmy Savile writes in *The People*: "The Stones are a great team for having a laugh and dress very clean and smart when they relax, contrary to what lots of people think . . ."
May	12	Group refused lunch at a Bristol hotel because they are not wearing ties. Headline: ROLLING STONES GATHER NO LUNCH (*Daily Express*).
May	15	Trentham Gardens, Stoke On Trent.
May	17	Odeon, Edmonton.

May	18	Glasgow.
May	23	Leicester University.
May	25	East Ham Granada with Peter and Gordon.
May	27	Reported that eleven boys have suspended from Woodlands Comprehensive School, Coventry, for wearing Mick Jagger hair cuts.
June	3	Leave for first US tour (ending June 23).
June	5	Record *Hollywood Palace* TV show.
June	10–12	Recording sessions at Chess studios in Chicago.
June	16	Fly back to Britain for just one night to appear at Magdalen College, Oxford, to honour a year-old booking for a £100 fee – their fares cost £1,500.
June	23	Riots at London Airport when they return home from US tour.
June	26	*It's All Over Now/Good Times, Bad Times* released by Decca. All-night *Welcome Home Stones* concert at Alexandra Palace.
July	4	Much-criticised appearance on BBC TV series *Juke Box Jury* – slated for mumbling, slovenly appearance and long hair.
July	8	*It's All Over Now* becomes their first Number One hit. Keith, Bill and Brian join the Beatles for a party at the Dorchester Hotel to celebrate the premiere of film *A Hard Day's Night*.
July	24	Empress Ballroom, Blackpool. Four youths arrested during riot which starts when Keith aims a kick at a youth who runs on stage. Thirty fans treated in hospital. Damage totals £2,000.

July	26	Record for *Thank Your Lucky Stars* TV series.
July	31	Belfast concert called off after twelve minutes because of rioting audience. Hysterical girls carried out in straight jackets.
August	3	Concert at the Marquess of Bath's home, Longleat, with 25,000 crowd. Over 200 girls faint.
August	7	Return to Richmond to star in the annual Jazz and Blues Festival.
August	8	Door torn off their car during riot after their appearance on *Ready, Steady, Go!* TV series.
August	9	Belle Vue, Manchester. Fifty police needed to control crowd. 100 girls faint, and so do two policewomen.
August	10	Mick Jagger fined £32 at Liverpool for driving without insurance, failing to produce his driving licence, and exceeding speed limit. Solicitor explains that he had been on an "errand of mercy" driving to hospital to see two fans injured in a car crash.
August	13	Palace ballroom, Douglas, Isle of Man, with crowd of 7,000.
August	14	Wimbledon Palais. Decca release *Five By Five* EP, which has advance orders of 200,000. Tracks: *If You Need Me/ Empty Heart/2120 South Michigan Avenue/Confessin' The Blues/Around and Around.*
August	18–20	New Theatre Ballroom, Guernsey, Channel Islands.
August	21–22	Springfield Hall, St. Helier, Jersey, Channel Islands.

August	23	Gaumont, Bournemouth.
August	24	Gaumont, Weymouth.
August	25	Odeon, Weston-Super-Mare.
August	26	ABC, Exeter.
August	27	ABC, Plymouth.
August	28	Gaumont, Taunton.
August	29	Town Hall, Torquay.
August	30	Return to Gaumont, Bournemouth.
September	5	Begin tour with The Mojos and Inez and Charlie Fox at Finsbury Park Astoria. Voted Britain's most popular rock group in *Melody Maker*. *Not Fade Away* voted best song.
September	6	Leicester Odeon.
September	8	Odeon, Colchester.
September	9	Odeon, Luton.
October	9	Announced that they have cancelled plans to tour South Africa after discussions with Musicians Union, who have embargo on musicians touring there because of apartheid policy.
October	14	Charlie Watts marries Shirley Ann Shepherd in Bradford.
October	16–17	Berlin TV show.
October	18–21	Fly to Brussels for Belgian TV show, and then to Paris for Olympia concert.
October	20	First show at Paris Olympia. Riots in street after show. Police make 150 arrests. Damage to theatre totals £1,400.
October	22	Fly back to London for one day at home before American tour.
October	23	Fly to US.
October	24	New York Academy of Music.
October	25	Debut on Ed Sullivan TV show.
October	26	Sacramento.
October	27	Off.

October	28–29	Film Tami Awards TV show with Gerry and the Pacemakers, Billy J. Kramer, Beach Boys, Four Seasons, Chuck Berry, Marvin Gaye and the Miracles, The Supremes.
October	30	San Francisco.
October	31	San Bernardino.
November	1	Municipal Hall, Long Beach.
November	2	Records *Shindig* TV show for Jack Good. Then record at RCA Studios. Co-manager Eric Easton taken ill with pneumonia and flown back to London.
November	3	Cleveland, Ohio.
November	4	Providence, Rhode Island.
November	5	Fly to Milwaukee and spend two days recording at the Chess studios in Chicago, followed by holiday.
November	12	Kingston, Ontario.
November	13	Detroit. In Britain, Decca rush release *Little Red Rooster/Off The Hook* with advance orders of 300,000. A-side was written by rhythm 'n' blues veteran Willie Dixon and had been a big hit in 1963 in the US for Sam Cooke.
November	14	Louisville.
November	15	Chicago.
November	16	Fly back to London.
November	23	Banned by the BBC after arriving late for radio shows *Saturday Club* and *Top Gear*.
November	27	Mick Jagger fined £16 for driving offences at Tettenhall, Staffs. His solicitor tells the Court: "Put out of your mind this nonsense talked about these young men. They are not long-haired idiots but highly intelligent university men . . . the

Duke of Marlborough had much longer hair than my client and he won some famous battles. His hair was powdered, I think because of fleas – my client has no fleas!"

November	29	Refuse to appear at ABC TV press reception in Birmingham.
November	30	Morning headlines: "THE ROLLING STONES RUN INTO NEW TELE-VISION ROW" (*Daily Mirror*), "THE STONES SNUB A PARTY" (*Sun*), "ROLLING STONES WALK OUT ON TV RECEPTION" (*Daily Express*).
December	6	Co-manager Andrew Oldham told he cannot appear on radio because of BBC dispute with the Stones.
December	12	Brian Jones denies rumours that he is quitting the group.

1965

January	1	Charlie Watts' book *Ode To A High Flying Bird* (a tribute to jazzman Charlie Parker) published.
January	6	Fly to Ireland for concerts in Dublin, Belfast and Cork.
January	10	Commodore, Hammersmith.
January	11–12	Recording.
January	13	Film item for *Thank Your Lucky Stars*.
January	15	*Ready, Steady, Go!* Second LP released by Decca, *The Rolling Stones No. 2*. Tracks: *Everybody Needs Somebody To Love/Down Home Girl/You Can't Catch Me/Time Is On My Side/What A Shame/Grown Up Wrong/Down The Road Apiece/Under The Boardwalk/I Can't Be*

Satisfied/Pain In My Heart/Off The Hook.

January	17	Fly to Los Angeles for recording sessions.
January	19	Fly from Los Angeles to Sydney, Australia, via Honolulu and Fiji.
January	21	Arrive in Sydney for tour with Roy Orbison, Rolf Harris and Dionne Warwick. Crowd of 3,000 waiting at airport.
January	22	Manufacturers Stadium, Sydney.
January	23	Sydney.
January	24	Fly to Brisbane.
January	25	Concerts and TV, Brisbane.
January	27	Sydney concerts.
January	28–30	Palais Theatre, Melbourne.
January	31	Leave for New Zealand.
February	1	Theatre Royal, Christchurch.
February	2	Civic Theatre, Invercargill.
February	3	Town Hall, Dunedin.
February	4	Fly to Auckland.
February	5	Off.
February	6	Town Hall, Auckland (three shows).
February	7	Off.
February	8	Barred by the Midland Hotel, Wellington, after crowd scenes elsewhere on tour.
February	9	Fly back to Melbourne.
February	10	Palais Theatre, Melbourne.
February	11	Centennial Hall, Adelaide.
February	12	Off.
February	13	Capitol Theatre, Perth.
February	14	Off.
February	15	Fly to Singapore.
February	16	Singapore concerts (two).
February	17–18	Cross the dateline flying via Tokyo and Honolulu to Los Angeles.
February	26	*The Last Time/Play With Fire* released –

the first time Mick and Keith had written an A-side. Mick mobbed by fans on *Ready, Steady, Go!* set and injures ankle.

March	5	Begin two-week British tour with the Hollies and Dave Berry at the Regal, Edmonton.
March	6	Empire Theatre, Liverpool.
March	7	Palace Theatre, Manchester. Girl falls from balcony during concert and is injured.
March	9	Odeon, Sunderland.
March	10	ABC, Huddersfield.
March	11	City Hall, Sheffield.
March	12	Granada, Rugby.
March	13	Odeon, Rochester.
March	14	Portsmouth.
March	15	Odeon, Guildford.
March	16	Granada, Greenford.
March	17	Odeon, Chelmsford.
March	18	ABC, Romford. Incident at filling station after the show.

March 24–		
April	5	Scandinavian tour.
April	9	*Ready, Steady, Go!* (live).
April	11	*New Musical Express* Poll Winners' Concert, Wembley.
April	13–16	German TV show and concerts.
April	17–18	Olympia Theatre, Paris.
April	22	Fly to Montreal to start North American tour.
April	23	Montreal.
April	24	Ottawa.
April	25	Maple Leaf Gardens, Toronto.
April	26	London, Ontario.
April	30	Worcester. Massachusetts.

May	1	New York Academy of Music.
May	2	Ed Sullivan TV show.
May	4	Statesboro, Georgia.
May	6	Municipal Auditorium, Atlanta, Georgia
May	8	The Coliseum, Jacksonville, Florida.
May	9	Aire Crown Theatre, Chicago.
May	10–11	Recording at Chess studios, Chicago.
May	12–13	Recording at RCA studios in Los Angeles.
May	14	Civic Auditorium, San Francisco.
May	15	Swing Auditorium, San Bernardino, California.
May	16	Civic Hall, Long Beach.
May	17	Convention Hall, San Diego.
May	18	Off.
May	19	Off.
May	20	Record *Shindig* TV show with Jack Good.
May	21	Civic Auditorium, San Jose.
May	22	Radcliff Convention Hall, Fresno.
May	23	Municipal Hall, Sacramento.
June	10	*Top Of The Pops.*
June	11	*Got Live If You Want It* EP released by Decca. Tracks: *We Want The Stones/ Everybody Needs Somebody To Love/ Pain In My Heart/Route 66/I'm Moving On/I'm Alright.*
June	12	*Thank Your Lucky Stars* TV show.
June	15	Begin brief Scottish tour at Odeon, Glasgow.
June	16	Usher Hall, Edinburgh.
June	17	Caird Hall, Dundee – forty girls faint.
June	18	Odeon, Aberdeen.
June	24–29	Scandinavian tour.
June	29	Charlie buys 16th century Sussex home from Lord Shawcross; the house once

		belonged to an Archbishop of Canterbury.
July	1	Glasgow magistrate describes the Stones as "animals, clowns and morons" after one of their fans has been arrested for breaking a shop window. Two Members of Parliament publicly defend the group.
July	7	Fly to Los Angeles for recording sessions
July	16	Odeon, Exeter, with Walker Brothers and Steam Packet.
July	17	Guildhall, Portsmouth.
July	18	Gaumont, Bournemouth.
July	22	Mick, Bill and Brian each fined £5 at West Ham plus costs for insulting behaviour at the filling station on March 18th. Court told that Bill used disgusting language in asking to use toilet – and then they urinated against the filling station wall. Magistrate says: "Because you have reached an exalted height in your profession, it does not mean you can behave in this manner."
July	25	Great Yarmouth.
August	1	London Palladium concert with the Walker Brothers and Steam Packet.
August	20	*I Can't Get No Satisfaction/The Spider and The Fly* released in Britain after already selling over 1,000,000 in US.
August	22	Futurist, Scarborough.
August	24	Stones meet Allen Klein for the first time at the Hilton Hotel, London.
August	28	Announced that The Stones have appointed Allen Klein and Andrew Oldham their co-managers, and Tito Burns their new agent, and also signed a new

recording contract with Decca who will also finance their first films.

September		*Out Of Our Heads* LP released by Decca. Tracks: *She Said Yeah/Mercy Mercy/ Hitch Hike/That's How Strong My Love Is/Good Times/Gotta Get Away/Talkin' 'Bout You/Cry To Me/Oh, Baby – We Got A Good Thing Going/Heart of Stone/The Under Assistant West Coast Promotion Man/I'm Free.*
September	3	Dublin.
September	4	Belfast.
September	8	Make what they announce as their last ballroom appearance at Douglas, Isle of Man.
September	10	Star in their own edition of Ready, Steady, Go!
September	11–17	Riots in Dusseldorf when Stones arrive for German tour. 70 people injured in West Berlin, and Berlin Hilton cancels their reservations.
September	25	Begin British tour with Spencer Davis, Mike Sarne and John Leyton at Southampton Gaumont.
September	26	Colston, Bristol.
September	27	Odeon, Cheltenham.
September	28	Capitol, Cardiff.
September	29	Granada, Shrewsbury.
September	30	Gaumont, Hanley.
October	1	ABC, Chester.
October	2	ABC, Wigan.
October	3	Odeon, Manchester.
October	4	Gaumont, Bradford.
October	5	ABC, Carlisle.
October	6	Odeon, Glasgow.
October	7	City Hall, Newcastle.

October	8	ABC, Stockton On Tees.
October	9	Odeon, Leeds.
October	10	Empire Theatre, Liverpool.
October	11	Odeon, Sheffield.
October	13	De Montfort, Leicester.
October	14	Odeon, Birmingham.
October	15	ABC, Cambridge.
October	16	Odeon, Southend.
October	17	Granada, Tooting.
October	22	*Get Off My Cloud*/*The Singer Not The Song* released by Decca.
October	29	Leave for Montreal for start of fourth US tour.
October	30	New York and Syracuse.
October	31	Toronto.
November	3	Providence, Rhode Island.
November	4	New Haven, Connecticut.
November	5	Boston.
November	6	New York Academy of Music and Philadelphia Convention Hall.
November	7	Mosque Theatre, Newark.
November	10	Reynolds Coliseum, Raleigh, North Carolina.
November	12	Greensboro, North Carolina.
November	13	Washington, DC and Baltimore.
November	14	Knoxville, Tennessee.
November	15	Charlotte, North Carolina.
November	16	Nashville, Tennessee.
November	17	Memphis, Tennessee.
November	19	Jackson, Mississipi.
November	20	Houston, Texas.
November	21	Fort Worth, Texas.
November	23	Tulsa, Oklahoma.
November	24	Pittsburgh, Pennsylvania.
November	25	Columbus, Ohio.
November	26	Detroit, Michigan.

November	27	Dayton, Ohio, and Cincinatti, Ohio.
November	28	Chicago, Illinois.
November	29	Denver, Colorado.
November	30	Scottsdale, Arizona.
December	1	Vancouver.
December	2	Seattle, Washington.
December	3	Sacramento. Electric shock knocks Keith unconscious.
December	4	San Jose. Brian Jones denies reports that he is to marry Anita Pallenberg.
December	5	Sports Arena, Los Angeles.
December	6	Begin recording schedule in Los Angeles.
December	31	*The New Year Starts Here* (Rediffusion TV special).

1966

February	4	*19th Nervous Breakdown/As Tears Go By* released by Decca.
February	12	Press reports that a fan committed suicide when his guardian told him to cut his hair. Stones fly to New York.
February	13	Ed Sullivan TV show.
February	14	Fly to Sydney for tours of Australia and New Zealand with concerts in Brisbane, Adelaide and in New Zealand, St. Kilda, Wellington and Auckland.
March	3	Begin recording schedule in Los Angeles.
March	25	Begin two-week European tour of Belgium, Holland, France, Germany, Sweden and Denmark.
March	26	Amsterdam.
March	27	Brussels.
March	28	Paris (TV show).
March	29	Olympia Theatre, Paris – 57 arrests, and Brigitte Bardot asks them to write her a song.

March	30	Marseilles – Mick has to have eight stitches after a chair is thrown at his head on stage.
March	31	Lyons.
April	2	Fly to Stockholm.
April	3	Tennishallen, Stockholm.
April	5	K.B. Hallen, Copenhagen.
April	6	Mick arrives back in London, still with black eye from that stage injury in Marseilles.
April	15	*Aftermath* LP released by Decca. All 14 tracks written by Mick and Keith. Tracks: *Mother's Little Helper/Stupid Girl/Lady Jane/Under My Thumb/ Doncha Bother Me/Goin' Home/Flight 505/Highland Dry/Out of Time/It's Not Easy/I Am Waiting/Take It Or Leave It/ Think/What To Do.*
May	1	*New Musical Express* Poll Winners Concert.
May	13	*Thank Your Lucky Stars* TV show. Announced that the Stones are to make their first film *Only Lovers Left Alive.*
May	13	*Paint It Black/A Long, Long While* released by Decca.
May	27	*Ready, Steady, Go!*
June	14	Mick collapses from overwork and exhaustion soon after moving into new home near Regents Park. Stones say they are issuing 5,000,000 US dollar law suit after fourteen American hotels cancel their reservations, saying that this amounts to "discrimination on account of national origin" violating civil rights laws.

June	29	Begin 20-day North American tour in Montreal and Toronto.
July	2	New York.
July	8	Syracuse.
July	9	Detroit.
July	10	Chicago.
July	25	Hollywood Bowl.
July	26	San Francisco.
July	28	Honolulu.
August	3	Begin two-week recording schedule at RCA Studios in Los Angeles.
August	7	First British showing of their package film *Gather No Moss*.
September	8	Fly to Dusseldorf at start of German tour.
September	10	Appear on Ed Sullivan TV show in US, and *Ready, Steady, Go!* in Britain.
September	23	*Have You Seen Your Mother, Baby, Standing In The Shadow!/Who's Driving Your Plane?* released by Decca. Presented with twenty gold discs after opening concert of tour at Albert Hall, London. Commence tour with Ike and Tina Turner and the Yardbirds.
September	24	Odeon, Leeds.
September	25	Empire Theatre, Liverpool.
September	28	ABC, Manchester.
September	29	ABC, Stockton.
September	30	Odeon, Glasgow.
October	1	City Hall, Newcastle.
October	2	Gaumont, Ipswich.
October	6	Odeon, Birmingham.
October	7	*Ready, Steady, Go!* and Colston, Bristol.
October	8	Capitol, Cardiff.
October	9	Gaumont, Southampton.
October	29	Begin US Tour in Montreal.

November	*Big Hits* (*High Tide and Green Grass*) LP released by Decca. Tracks: *Have You Seen Your Mother, Baby, Standing In The Shadow?/Paint It Black/It's All Over Now/The Last Time/Heart of Stone/Not Fade Away/Come On/I Can't Get No Satisfaction/Get Off Of My Cloud/As Tears Go By/19th Nervous Breakdown/Lady Jane/Time Is On My Side/Little Red Rooster.*
November	*Got Live If You Want It!* LP released, with the same title as the earlier EP – this is a live recording of the Albert Hall concert. Tracks: *Under My Thumb/Get Off Of My Cloud/Lady Jane/Not Fade Away/I've Been Loving You Too Long/Fortune Teller/The Last Time/19th Nervous Breakdown/Time Is On My Side/I'm Alright/Have You Seen Your Mother, Baby, Standing In The Shadow?/I Can't Get N Satisfaction.*

1967

January	*Between The Buttons* LP released by Decca. Tracks: *Yesterday's Papers/My Obsession/Back Street Girl/Connection/She Smiles Sweetly/Cool Calm and Collected/All Sold Out/Please Go Home/Who's Been Sleeping Here?/Complicated/Miss Amanda Jones/Something Happened To My Yesterday.*
January 13	*Let's Spend The Night Together/Ruby Tuesday* single released by Decca.
January 14	Tape numbers for Ed Sullivan TV show.
January 22	*Sunday Night At The London Palladium* TV show. Stones mime to pre-recorded

music and refuse to appear on the roundabout at the end of the show, which causes press sensation. "They're insulting me and everyone else," said the show's director.

January	26	*Top Of The Pops* (BBC-1).
February	2	*Top Of The Pops* (BBC-1).
February	5	*Eamonn Andrews Show* (ABC TV).
February	6	Mick Jagger announces that he is taking legal action against the *News Of The World*.
February	12	Police raid Keith Richard's home at West Wittering during weekend party.
February	19	*News of the World* headlines story "DRUG SQUAD RAIDS POP STARS' PARTY".
February	23	Mick and Marianne Faithfull arrive eight minutes late for ballet at Royal Opera House – Rudolf Nureyev and Margot Fonteyn in world premiere of Roland Petit's *Paradise Lost*.
March	8	Mick becomes a Friend of Covent Garden Opera House.
March	9	Brian Jones enters hospital with respiratory trouble.
March	25	Begin European tour at Malmo, Sweden. Baggage searched by Customs. "They even went through our underclothes," said Mick Jagger.
March	26	Helsinki.
March	28	Orebro, Sweden. Police use batons and dogs to break up riot.
March	29	Fly to Germany for concerts in Hamburg, Berlin and Essen.
April	2	Vienna concert. 154 fans arrested.

154

April	5	Fly to Italy for concerts in Rome, Turin and Milan.
April	8	Daily Express quotes Olympic gold medallist Lynn Davies criticising Stones' behaviour in German hotel. Mick Jagger replies that "the accusations are disgusting and completely untrue. We deny that we were badly behaved. I cannot remember when we have behaved better. We hardly used the public rooms in this hotel. They were crammed with athletes behaving badly".
April	11	Olympia Theatre, Paris. 200 police to control crowds. Stones again searched by Customs. "I feel as if I am being treated as a witch," says Mick Jagger.
April	12	Mick punched by airport official in row at Le Bourget Airport while the Stones on their way to Warsaw.
April	13	First visit behind the Iron Curtain. 2,000 fans storm the Palace of Culture, Warsaw, when 7,000 are turned away. Police bring in dogs and then tear gas.
April	14	Zurich – Mick Jagger thrown to ground during riot.
April	15	Paris.
April	16	Bordeaux.
April	24	German entry to the Cannes Film Festival is *A Degree Of Murder* with music by Brian Jones and starring his girlfriend Anita Pallenberg.
May	10	Following the February 12 raid, Mick and Keith are prosecuted on drugs charges at Chichester and sent for trial at West Sussex Quarter Sessions on £100 bail. Brian Jones charged with being in

155

		possession of Indian hemp at his South Kensington flat.
May	11	Brian Jones appears in court and is remanded on £250 bail.
May	21	Mick appears on BBC *Look Of The Week* with Professor John Cohen of Manchester University to discuss relationships between performers and audiences.
June		*Flowers* LP released by Decca. Tracks: *Ruby Tuesday/Have You Seen Your Mother, Baby, Standing In The Shadow!/Let's Spend The Night Together/Lady Jane/Out Of Time/My Girl/Back Street Girl/Please Go Home/Mothers Little Helper/Take It Or Leave It/Ride On Baby/Sittin' On A Fence.*
June	29	Mick and Keith both found guilty at West Sussex Quarter Sessions. Mick is sentenced to three months in gaol with £100 costs and Keith to a year in gaol with £500 costs. Mick taken to Brixton Gaol for the night; Keith to Wormwood Scrubs.
June	30	Mick and Keith each given £7,000 bail in the High Court.
July	1	Famous editorial in *The Times* headed BUTTERFLY ON A WHEEL?
July	2	In *The Sunday Express*, John Gordon writes: "Was Jagger convicted of taking one of the evil drugs like heroin, or cocaine? Or LSD with which some of the Beatles confess that they have been experimenting? Not at all. Did he smoke marijuana which some experts say is evil, but others, equally expert, say is not so

evil? That wasn't alleged against him. He merely had four benzedrine tablets, legally purchased abroad, which, with the knowledge and approval of his doctor, he took to keep him awake while he worked . . . I repeat, have we lost our sense of proportion?"

July	6	Brian Jones in hospital suffering from strain.
July	31	Lord Chief Justice hears appeals by Mick and Keith. Keith's conviction is quashed; Mick is given a conditional discharge.
August	18	*We Love You/Dandelion* released by Decca. Lennon and McCartney sing backing harmonies.
August	26	Mick Jagger and Marianne Faithfull go off with the Beatles to meet the Maharishi at a convention in Wales.
September		Stones go to the States, and announce on their return at the end of the month that they have broken away from Andrew Oldham and will in future produce their own records.
October	14	Reported in *Melody Maker* that Mick has turned down part in film *The Virgin Soldiers*.
October	21	Mick Jagger denies national press reports that the Stones may build their own recording studios in partnership with the Beatles.
October	31	Brian Jones sentenced to nine months in gaol for possessing cannabis, and is later released on £750 bail pending appeal.
December	8	*Their Satanic Majesties Request* LP released by Decca. Tracks: *Sing This All*

*Together/Citadel/In Another World/2000
Man/Sing This All Together (See What
Happens)/She's A Rainbow/The Lantern/
Gomper/2000 Light Years From Home/
On With The Show.*

December	12	Brian Jones appeals and his gaol sentence is set aside. Instead he is fined £1,000 and placed on probation for three years.
December	15	Brian Jones admitted to St. George's Hospital after collapsing; said to be "tired and suffering from overstrain".
December	16	Announced that the Stones are to launch their own record label with the name Mother Earth.

1968

January	4	Reported in the Daily Sketch that the University of California is insisting that students taking music degrees must study the Stones' music as the music professor feels they have made an important contribution to modern music.
March	2	Announced that American record producer Jimmy Miller is to work with the Stones. "Mick contacted me and said he liked the things I did with Traffic. He had been producing the Stones but says he doesn't want to be on two sides of the control room window now," says Miller.
March	15	Jimmy Miller produces first sessions with the Stones.
March	16	Brian Jones' girlfriend Linda Keith collapses at flat in Chesham Place, Belgravia.
March	17	Second Stones session with Jimmy

Miller, and during the night Charlie receives phone call to say wife is in labour.

March	18	Charlie and Shirley Watts' daughter Serafina born.
May	12	*New Musical Express* Poll Winners' Concert – Rolling Stones make their first British public appearance in two years.
May	21	Brian Jones arrested and charged with possessing cannabis. At Marlborough Street Magistrates Court he is given £2,000 bail.
May	25	*Jumping Jack Flash/Child of the Moon* released by Decca.
June		Rolling Stones work on film *One Plus One* with Jean Luc Godard.
June	11	Brian Jones committed for trial at Inner London Sessions. Fire breaks out at Olympic Studios while they are recording. No-one injured.
July	29	Mick Jagger begins filming *Performance*, playing a singer/social drop-out who comes into contact with a gangster, played by James Fox. The group then begins a long holiday – with Mick going to Ireland with Marianne; Brian Jones to Morocco to tape local folk music; Keith Richard to Los Angeles. Bill and Charlie stay at home.
September	6	Mick appears on David Frost's TV show. Group's latest US single *Street Fighting Man* banned by some radio stations because it might incite riots.
September	26	Brian Jones fined £50 with £105 costs at Inner London Sessions after being

		found guilty of possessing cannabis.

November   21   Brian Jones buys A. A. Milne's former home, Cotchford Farm near Hartfield, Sussex.

December   5   Stones hold 'beggars banquet' in London to mark the release of their *Beggars Banquet* album. Lord Harlech deputises for Keith Richard who is ill, and they surprise guests with a custard pie throwing finale. Tracks: *Sympathy For The Devil/No Exception/Dear Doctor/Parachute Woman/Jig-saw Puzzle/Street Fighting Man/Prodigal Son/Stray Cat Blues/Factory Girl/Salt of the Earth.*

December 10–12   Filming *Rock and Roll Circus* with John and Yoko Lennon, Eric Clapton and Jethro Tull.

December   18   Mick and Keith leave for Brazil with Marianne Faithfull and Anita Pallenberg; Brian goes on holiday to Ceylon.

1969

January   17   Mick and Keith asked to leave the Hotel Crillon in Lima because they were wearing op art trousers and nothing else. They move to the Hotel Bolivar.

May   24   Mick and Marianne charged in London with possessing cannabis and allowed £50 bail.

May   28   Announced that Mick Jagger will play title role in forthcoming *Ned Kelly* film to be produced in Australia.

June   8   Brian Jones leaves the Rolling Stones. "I no longer see eye to eye with the others over the discs we are cutting," he says.

Jun	13	Press conference and photocall in Hyde Park to announce that Mick Taylor, formerly with John Mayall, is joining the Stones in Brian's place as lead guitarist.
June	25–26	Rome Coliseum.
July	3	Brian Jones found dead in the swimming pool at his Sussex home, Cotchford Farm.
July	4	*Honky Tonk Women/You Can't Always Get What You Want*. The Stones' first single for 14 months with Mick Taylor playing guitar on both sides.
July	5	Free concert in Hyde Park attended by 250,000 people. Mick Jagger reads a dedication to Brian from a poem by Shelley and then thousands of butterflies are released.
July	6	Mick Jagger leaves for Australia to film *Ned Kelly*. Announced that Marianne Faithfull's husband John Dunbar is suing her for divorce citing Mick Jagger.
July	8	Marianne in coma, and is subsequently replaced in the film.
July	9	Brian Jones' funeral.
August	10	Keith Richard's son Marlon born.
August	18	Mick injured in the hand in shooting accident on the *Ned Kelly* film set.
September		*Through The Past Darkly* LP released by Decca, collection of past hits packaged in memory of Brian. Tracks: *Jumpin' Jack Flash/Mothers Little Helper/2000 Light Years From Home/Let's Spend The Night Together/You Better Move On/ We Love You/Street Fighting Man/ She's A Rainbow/Ruby Tuesday/Dan-*

161

delion/*Sittin' On The Fence*/*Honky Tonk Women*.

September	12	Mick Jagger returns from Australia.
October	17	Stones fly to Los Angeles for US tour running through to mid-December.
November	13	In Dallas, Texas, Mick denies reports that he and Marianne are breaking up.
December		*Let It Bleed* LP released by Decca. Tracks: *Gimme Shelter*/*Love In Vain*/*Country Honk*/*Live With Me*/*Let It Bleed*/*Midnight Rambler*/*You Got The Silver*/*Monkey Man*/*You Can't Always Get What You Want*.
December	6	Altamont – a member of the audience trying to get to the stage is stabbed to death by Hells Angels.
December	7	San Francisco. Chaos as fans abandon cars, buses and vans in traffic jams to make their way on foot to the concert.
December	14	Saville Theatre, London.
December	19	Mick fined £200 with £52.50 costs at Marlborough Street Magistrates Court on cannabis charge. Marianne Faithfull acquitted.
December	21	Lyceum, London.

1970

January	31	Rolling Stones file a £4,580,000 law suit in the States suing Sears Point International Raceway for breach of contract and fraud claiming that they had to move at the last moment to Altamont Raceway nearly 40 miles away for the December 6 concert.
July	28	Premiere of *Ned Kelly* in Melbourne, Australia.

July	30	Rolling Stones inform Allen Klein that "neither he nor ABKCO Industries Inc nor any other company have any authority to negotiate recording contracts on their behalf in the future".
August	1	*Performance* film released starring Mick Jagger, Anita Pallenberg and James Fox.
August	29	Rolling Stones begin six-week European tour.
September	4	Royal Tennis Hall, Stockholm. Hundreds of fans storm the stage.
September	8	*Get Your Ya Yas Out!* LP released. Live album of 1969 US tour released to counter-act success of bootleg LP in the States. Tracks: *Jumpin' Jack Flash/ Carol/Stray Cat Blues/Love In Vain Midnight Rambler/Sympathy For The Devil/Live With Me/Little Queenie/ Honky Tonk Women/Street Fighting Man.*
September	14	Ernst Merck Halle, Hamburg. 200 police on duty to cope with crowds after 1,000 forged tickets have been issued before the concert.
September	16	Deutschlandhalle, Berlin. 50 people arrested in disturbances before the show.
September	19	*Performance* soundtrack LP released, featuring Mick Jagger, Randy Newman, Ry Cooder and Buffy St Marie.
September	23	Olympia Theatre, Paris. Police injured in fights. Demand for tickets so great that two extra concerts were arranged at the Palais Des Sports.
October	1	Palazzo del Sport, Milan. Police use tear gas to disperse crowd of 2,000.

		Seven police injured and 63 people arrested.
October	7	*Ned Kelly* film released in Britain.
November	7	Mick Jagger solo from the film *Performance – Memo To Turner/Natural Magic* – released as a single.
December	6	*Gimme Shelter* (film of 1969 US tour) opens in New York.

1971

January	4	Keith Richard attends London charity premiere of *Performance* (his girlfriend Anita Pallenberg played opposite Jagger in the film).
February	22	Hundreds of fans sleep on the pavement in Sauchihall Street, Glasgow, waiting for the box office to open for concert on March 8.
March	1	Fans stampede outside Liverpool Empire Theatre waiting for box office to open.
March	2	*A Story of Our Time – Brian Jones, the Rolling Stone* on Radio 4 (BBC).
March	4	Rolling Stones announce that they will be leaving England to live in France. Estimated in *The Daily Telegraph* that they have earned an estimated £83,000,000 over past nine years, and will save considerably on tax by the move. Announcement is made in Newcastle Upon Tyne where they appeared at the City Hall.
March	8	Green's Playhouse, Glasgow.
March	14	Farewell Concert at the Roundhouse, London. Ticket touts charge up to £10 for tickets.
March	30	Rolling Stones give farewell party at

164

Skindles Hotel, Maidenhead. Guests include John and Yoko Lennon, David Bailey and Eric Clapton.

April	1	Announced that Marshall Chess will be running their new label, Rolling Stones Records.
April	6	In Cannes, Stones sign a distribution deal for Rolling Stones Records with the Kinney Group.
April	13	*Brown Sugar/Bitch/Let It Rock* maxi-single is their first release on the new Rolling Stones Record label.
April	16	Mick and Bianca visit the Philippe Tallien art gallery in St Tropez.
April	18	Mick and Bianca photographed leaving the Yves St Laurent boutique in St Tropez. They deny rumours that they are to marry.
April	23	*Sticky Fingers* is their first LP on their new label, with a cover specially designed by Andy Warhol. Tracks: *Brown Sugar/ Sway/Wild Horses/Can't You Hear Me Knocking/You Gotta Move/Bitch/. Got The Blues/Sister Morphine/Dead Flowers/Moonlight Mile.* *Stone Age* LP is released by Decca with four tracks previously unreleased – *Look What You've Done/One More Try/My Girl/Blue Turns To Grey.*
May	2	Bianca's birthday – Mick goes to Paris and buys her a £4,000 bracelet and arranges a dinner party for her.
May	3	*Brown Sugar* reaches No. 1 in charts.
May	8	Mick goes to Paris to collect two specially designed wedding rings ordered from a top French jeweller.

May	12	Mick Jagger marries Bianca Perez Morena de Macias in St Tropez at a civil ceremony at the Town Hall followed by blessing at the Chapel of St Anne. (Mick had spent previous two weeks taking Roman Catholic religious instruction.) Guests at the wedding included their families and the Stones plus Ringo and Maureen Starr, Ronnie Lane, Ian McLagen, Ronnie Wood, Kenny Jones, Roger Vadim, John Walker, Nathalie Delon, Ahmet Ertegun, Marshall Chess, Ossie Clark, Jimmy Miller, Lord Kitchfield and Lord Brooks.
May	13	After all-night party, Mick and Bianca leave Cannes in a yacht for their honeymoon.
May	24	*The Stones In The Park* is shown for the first time on Granada TV in colour.
May	30	Mick and Bianca return to St Tropez.
June	2	Mick and Bianca go to Venice.
July	2	Tucky Buzzard group release *She's A Striker*, produced by Bill Wyman.
July	30	Passing through Heathrow en route to Ireland for a short holiday at Leixlip Castle as guests of the Guinness family, Mick and Bianca announce that they are expecting a baby.
July	31	Premiere of *Gimme Shelter* at the Rialto Cinema, London.
August	5	Mick Jagger, speaking from France on the results of the OZ trial in London: "If there has been a moral crime committed then it is that by the police and the judge. It is impossible to shut a people or a

generation off from that which they wish
to read."

August	20	Howlin' Wolf LP on which Bill Wyman and Charlie Watts worked in the studios released on the Rolling Stones Records label.
August	27	*Gimme Shelter* LP released by Decca. Collection of previously released material.
September	23	Mick and Bianca attend the Johnny Halliday concert at the Palais des Sports and then a party afterwards at Maxim's.
October	1	Thieves steal eleven guitars from Keith's house in France, and he offers a reward.
October	8	The album of Moroccan folk music recorded by Brian Jones shortly before he died released under the title *Joujouka* on the Rolling Stones Records label.
October	21	Mick and Bianca's daughter Jade born at the Belvedere nursing home in Paris.
October	26	Mick featured in ATV programme *Beaton By Bailey*.
November	3	Mick and Bianca attend Pierre Cardin's Paris party for Alice Cooper.
November	30	Mick and Keith leave for the States with Keith en route to Nashville where he is having guitars made to replace those that were stolen.

1972

February	1	Mick and Bianca attend the San Francisco wedding of John Phillips (formerly with the Mamas and the Papas) and Genevieve Waite.
		Stones spend much of February recording in Los Angeles.

February	29	Mick attends the Marc Bolan concert at the Hollywood Palladium.
April	6	Mick, Bianca and Jade stay over in Sydney en route to Bali for three-week holiday.
April	14	*Tumblin' Dice/Sweet Black Angel* single released on Rolling Stones Records label.
April	27	Bianca attends the Zandra Rhodes fashion show at the Roundhouse, London.
May	5	Bill and Charlie attend Wilson Pickett reception at WEA offices, London.
May	9	Rolling Stones and ABKCO Industries Inc., and Allen Klein jointly announce settlement of all outstanding differences.
May	12	*Exile On Main Street* LP released on Rolling Stones Records label. Tracks: *Rocks Off/Rip This Joint/Shake Your Hips/Casino Boogie/Tumbling Dice/ Sweet Virginia/Torn and Frayed/Sweet Black Angel/Loving Cup/Happy/Turd On The Run/Ventilator Blues/I Just Want to See His Face/Let It Loose/All Down The Line/Stop Breaking Down/Shine A Light/ Soul Survivor.*
May	16	Bianca Jagger models hairstyles and wigs for Ricci Burns at Oxfam Maytime Fair at Grosvenor House, London.
May	21	Begin rehearsals for US tour.
May	23	Rolling Stones attend personally at the US Embassy, London, to collect their work permits – and all except Bill miss their plane to New York and then LA.
May	25	Bianca sees Mick, Keith and Mick Taylor off at London Airport.
June	3	Begin North American tour with Stevie

168

Wonder and Martha Reeves at the Pacific Coliseum, Vancouver. 30 police are injured as 2,000 people try to gate-crash the concert.

June	4	Coliseum, Seattle.
June	5	Off.
June	6	Winterland, San Francisco.
June	7	Off.
June	8	Winterland, San Francisco.
June	9	Palladium, Los Angeles.
June	10	Pacific Terrace Center, Long Beach.
June	11	Forum, Los Angeles.
June	12	Off.
June	13	International Sports Arena, San Diego, California. 60 people arrested. 15 injured.
June	14	Civic Arena, Tucson, Arizona. Police use tear gas to disperse 200–300 youths who try to gatecrash the concert.
June	15	University of New Mexico, Albuquerque Forged ticket scare – and six people faint when others rush for their seats.
June	16	Coliseum, Denver.
June	17	Off.
June	18	Sports Center, Minneapolis.
June	19–20	Ampitheatre, Chicago.
June	21	Off.
June	22	Muncipal Auditorium, Kansas.
June	23	Off.
June	24	Tarrant County, Fort Worth, Texas.
June	25	Hoffeinz Pavilion, Houston, Texas.
June	26	Off.
June	27	Auditorium, Mobile, Alabama.
June	28	University of Alabama, Tuscaloosa.
June	29	Municipal Auditorium, Nashville.
June	30	Off. In London, Decca release maxi sin-

gle *Street Fighting Man/Surprise Surprise/Everybody Needs Somebody to Love*.

July	1–3	Off.
July	4	RFK Stadium, Washington DC. Crowd of 48,000 with 61 arrests.
July	5	Scope, North Oak, Virginia.
July	6	Coliseum, Charlotte, North Carolina.
July	7	Civic Arena, Knoxville, Tennessee.
July	8	Off.
July	9	Kiel Auditorium, St Louis, Missouri.
July	10	Off.
July	11	Rubber Bowl, Acron, Ohio.
July	12	Convention Center, Indianapolis.
July	13–14	Cobo Hall, Detroit.
July	15	Maple Leaf Gardens, Toronto.
July	16	Off.
July	17	Forum, Montreal. Riot after discovery that 3,000 fake tickets have been sold. Replacements flown from LA when Stones equipment was damaged by a bomb.
July	18–19	Boston Garden, Boston, Massachusetts.
July	20–21	Spectrum, Philadelphia.
July	22	Pittsburgh, Pennsylvania.
July	23	Off.
July	24–26	Madison Square Gardens, New York. After final concert, Mick hosts birthday party at St Regis Hotel.
August	10–11	Mick and Bianca Jagger at the Oval for Test Match.
August	11	Dick Cavett devotes two-thirds of his TV show to the Rolling Stones.
August	28	Mick and Bianca begin holiday in Ireland staying at the Earl of Gowrie's home near The Curragh.

September	22	Mick Jagger, Bianca, Charlie and Shirley Watts, and Mick Taylor attend party at the WEA Offices for their personal secretary Shirley Arnold who is leaving after nine years with the Rolling Stones.
November	6	Bill Wyman banned from driving and fined £20 for speeding by magistrates at Chelmsford.
November	8	Bianca Jagger wins "Woman of the Year" hat award and attends luncheon at the Inn On The Park Hotel, London, to receive the award.
November 22–24		Mick Jagger in New York to help Yoko Ono record her solo album with assistance from husband John Lennon.
November	25	Rolling Stones arrive in Jamaica for recording sessions that produce *Goat's Head Soup* LP.
December	21	Jamaican recording sessions completed.
December	23	Earthquake in Managua, Nicaragua. Bianca in a state of shock at the Jaggers home because her family live in Managua.
December	26	Mick and Bianca Jagger leave Heathrow en route for Nicaragua to search for Bianca's mother and other relations.
December	28	Mick and Bianca charter jet for final stage from Kingston, Jamaica, and take in with them 2,000 typhoid injection capsules. While searching in Managua, they find Mrs Macias and other members of Bianca's family.

1973

January	3	In an American poll of 200 international fashion experts, Mick and Bianca both

voted among the top dressed men and women of 1972.

January	4	Mick and Bianca reported safe after being missing for 48 hours in Nicaragua.
January	10	Mick Jagger says in Los Angeles that he would like to hold a benefit concert for victims of the Nicaraguan earthquake.
January	18	The charity concert is staged at the Forum, Los Angeles, and raises £200,000 for the earthquake victims.
January	21–22	International Sports Centre, Honolulu (two concerts).
February	8	The Rolling Stones arrive in Sydney at start of their Australian and New Zealand tour.
February	9	Press reception in Sydney.
February	11	More than 30,000 people attend concert at Western Springs Stadium, Auckland, New Zealand.
February	13	Milton Park Tennis Courts, Brisbane. In Auckland about £550 is raised for a local boys' recreation centre by the auction of bed linen used by the group.
February	16	Press concert at the Montsaluat Castle, Melbourne.
February	17–18	Kooyong Tennis Courts, Melbourne (two concerts).
February	20–21	Memorial Park Drive, Adelaide. After second concert, 21 people are arrested when 5,000 fans clash with police.
February	24	Western Australia Cricket Ground, Perth.
February	26–27	Royal Randwick Racecourse, Sydney. When the tour finishes, the group go off

		on holiday – Bill to America, Charlie to France, Keith to Jamaica, Mick Taylor to Indonesia and Mick Jagger to Jamaica and then to US.
April	7	*The Rolling Stones Story* starts on BBC Radio 1.
April	29	*Sad Day/You Can't Always Get What You Want* (two old recordings) released by their former recording company Decca.
April	30	Mick and Bianca attend New York party arranged by the magazine *After Dark* to present its second annual Ruby Award for the Entertainer of the Year to Bette Midler.
May	2	Portrait of Mick Jagger by Sir Cecil Beaton sold for £220 at Sotherby's.
May	9	Mick and Bianca fly to Washington to present the Senate with a £350,000 cheque towards the Pan American Development Fund. In return they are presented with a golden key as thanks for their January concert for the Nicaragua disaster victims.
May	11	Bianca Jagger attends the Liza Minnelli midnight concert at the London Palladium.
May	17	Mick and Bianca attend Ritz Hotel reception to launch GM records – Mick's younger brother Chris is one of the new label's first signings.
May	26	Mick and Bianca holiday on Scottish island of Gigha.
June	13	In American magazine *Cream*, the Stones are voted No. 1 Group, No. 1 Live Group and receive the award for

the Top LP (*Exile On Main Street*). Bill is voted Top Bass Player.

June	14	The Jimi Hendrix film documentary opens in London, including conversations between Jimi and Mick Jagger.
June	18	Mick, Bianca and Jade go to Italy for short holiday.
June	25	Mick Jagger goes to the Queen Elizabeth Hall, London, to see Mick Taylor performing with Mike Oldfield's Tubular Bells.
July	4	Mick and Bianca Jagger attend David Bowie at the Cafe Royal after Bowie's announcement that he is retiring from live concerts.
July	24–25	Bianca in Paris modelling Yves St Laurent clothes for the Daily Mirror.
July	30	Mick Jagger attends Test Match at the Oval.
July	31	At West Wittering, Sussex, Keith's house badly damaged by fire. Keith and Anita escape injury with their children, and manage to save books, antique furniture and equipment.
August	20	*Angie/Silver Train* single released on Rolling Stones Records label.
August	31	*Goat's Head Soup* LP released on Rolling Stones Records label. Tracks: *Dancing With Mr. D./100 Years Ago/Coming Down Again/Doo Doo Doo Doo Doo (Heartbreaker)/Angie/Silver Train/Hide Your Love/Winter/Can You Hear The Music/Star Star*.
September	1	First major European tour in three years opens at the Stadhalle in Vienna. Stones say it is one of their best-ever concerts.

| September | 7–9 | Empire Pool, Wembley, London. |
| October | 24 | Keith Richard fined a total of £205 by Marlborough Street Magistrate when he admits to having cannabis, Chinese heroin and Mandrax tablets plus a revolver, a shotgun and ammunition at his Chelsea home. Anita Pallenberg given a conditional discharge for a year for possessing 25 Mandrax tablets. Their lawyer says the drugs had been left at the house by other people who stayed there while Keith was out of the country. |

APPENDIX II

This was the official biography of the Rolling Stones, issued to national papers and the teenage magazines by the Decca press office in July, 1964, soon after the release of their first album and their first No. 1 hit *It's All Over Now*:

"It all started in the summer of '62. Brian Jones had his own group playing every Tuesday in an Ealing Club; among the fans were an up-and-coming vocalist Mick Jagger and guitarist Keith Richard. All three boys had one main interest, to put R & B on the map. This interest led to Mick and Keith joining the group. Soon after joining the three of them took a flat in Chelsea; the term "flat" was rather glamorous for it was a single room with no cooking or heating facilities. Things got worse; the pay at the club was not enough to keep them going – they started to flog bits and pieces of clothes and furniture in order to eat. Mick was living on his grant from the London School of Economics and Keith and Brian occasionally found jobs. Still this almost fanatic interest in R & B kept them going. They would practise regularly, experiment with different styles to interpret the uninhibited blues they played. Still the going was rough and they were soon left with a few treasured possessions, one being a record player on which they constantly played discs by artists like Chuck Berry, Bo Diddley, Little Walter and Jimmy Reed. Fish & Chips became the one meal of the day, with an occasional hot pie as a treat.

"The Stones carried on, and after a performance at the Scene Club on Boxing Day '63, they took on drummer Charlie Watts, bass guitarist Bill Wyman and Ian Stewart, who is now road manager, on piano and maraccas. With the new group, they decided to break into a fresh venture, that of promoters. They hired dance halls and took the money at the door. Suddenly it happened! Everywhere they played – The Marquee, Eel Pie Island, and the Ricky Tick Clubs – small numbers of R & B fans doubled then trebled. Everywhere they went the fans screamed for more, especially at the Station Hotel, Richmond, where the boys played every Sunday. Even the Beatles visited the Hotel to see the group that was causing the disturbance with their wild R & B. At that time a young man named Andrew Oldham, a live-wire publicist, was associated with the Beatles. Andrew or Andy as he prefers had been snowed under with work in connection with the boys. The amount of work involved turned it into a full-time job, but this was not for him – he wanted to have time to make records, find talent, and develop newcomers. The Beatles and several other people connected with the pop scene had talked about the Stones and Andy felt it called for a visit to Richmond. He was knocked out by them and with Eric Easton as co-manager, the Stones were signed on May 3rd, 1963. On May 10th they recorded a Chuck Berry number *Come On* and on June 7th Decca released the disc. The record proved to be a resounding success, although not reaching the top ten, it climbed to around the 18 mark and was in the charts for about four months.

"Meanwhile, the Stones were happy playing the Clubs. Their act was never formal – they sat around on stalls and just played and sang. Their gear was always casual. Then came the big opportunity – the boys were offered a tour with Bo Diddley, a man who was one of their greatest idols. It was decided for them, when they accepted the tour, that they would wear a vague sort of uniform. Shirts, ties, leather waistcoats and dog-tooth jackets were tried, but in the end they went back to casual clothes. They also gave up trying to keep their hair under control and it grew longer and longer.

"The next problem was a follow up disc. *Come On* had the whole music business submitting numbers to the Oldham office, but nothing was suited to the Stones' style. It was by chance that the Beatles, again, came on to the scene. Paul and John met up with Andy Oldham, and knowing of his difficulty to find a suitable new number for the boys, asked him if he thought that one of their songs *I Wanna Be Your Man* would be of any use. Andy asked them to sing it over, and immediately on hearing it dragged them into a taxi and tore down to Ken Colyer's Club where the Stones were rehearsing a few songs. They played over the number and the Stones were knocked out. The number was recorded and on November 1st it was released. The disc climbed steadily and was soon in the Top Ten, reaching No. 8 position.

"Their nation-wide popularity was increasing and the next disc *Not Fade Away*, an old Buddy Holly number, given a Bo Diddley-type backing by the Stones, went straight into the charts at number 10 and made the No. 3 spot. Their latest record earned a silver disc in the first week of release and is a sure-fire chart-topper. The number *It's All Over Now* was recorded by the boys in Chicago during their recent American tour, on which they played several big dates including the Carnegie Hall. The disc is a mid-tempo R & B offering, but completely different from their previous work. Apart from their singles the Stones have held the top position in the LP and EP Charts for a number of weeks. The boys' fantastic popularity is evident for they were recently voted No. 1 British vocal group in the Record Mirror poll.

"Dates include a Juke Box Jury appearance, a nation-wide ballroom tour, appearances in the Isle of Man, Guernsey and Jersey, followed by a five-week one-nighter in the autumn. 'We like to let the fans see us play as often as possible,' says Mick Jagger. 'That is why we tour so much.'

MICK JAGGER

"Mick (his real name is Michael Philip Jagger) was born in Dartford, Kent, on July 26th, 1944. He is 5ft 10ins tall, weighs 10st 6lbs, has blue eyes and brown hair. Was educated at Dartford Grammar School and the London School of Economics. He is the lead vocalist in the group, but also plays the harmonica. His taste in music is definitely R & B; his favourite artists include Solomon Burke, Bo Diddley, Chuck Berry and Jimmy Reed, likes driving alone through the night, yellow socks, money and females; doesn't like getting up, motorway cafes and intolerance. Eats well-cooked steaks. Hobbies include song-writing and tinkering about with boats. Clothes are always casual – a suit is a once a year treat.

BRIAN JONES
"Brian was born in Cheltenham in Gloucestershire on February 28th, 1944. He is 5ft 8ins tall and weighs 10st 11lb, has grey-green eyes and blond hair. Was educated at Cheltenham Grammar School. He plays both harmonica and a Gretsch semi-acoustic guitar; also joins Mick in vocals. His taste in music is also definitely R & B and h s favourite artists are Johnny Cash, Bo Diddley and Jimmy Reed. Likes having showers, cars, feminine girls, animals and sitting on mountains. Dislikes public transport, ants and cruelty. Likes casual clothes.

CHARLIE WATTS
"Charlie was born in Wembley, Middlesex, on June 2nd, 1941. He is 5ft 8 ins tall, weighs 10 stone, has grey eyes and brown hair. He was educated at Tylers Croft and Harrow Art College and plays drums. Likes modern jazz and R & B. His favourite artists include Buddy Greco and Sammy Davis. Likes Picasso, collecting antique gems, clothes and silver blondes. Dislikes nothing and nobody in particular. Clothes=suits, American and Continental gear – and is called by the others, the Beau Brummell of the group.

179

KEITH RICHARD

"Keith (real name Keith Richards) was born on December 18th, 1942. Educated at Dartford Technical School and then Sidcup Art School. Is 5ft 10ins tall, weighs 10st, has hazel eyes and black hair. Plays lead guitar (a Gibson). Taste in music: R & B and C & W. His favourite artists include Muddy Waters, The Shirelles, The Crystals and Chuck Berry. Likes sleeping, sketching, reading, boats and beautiful brunettes. Dislikes two-faced people and policemen. Wears casual clothes because he feels more comfortable.

BILL WYMAN

"Bill, born in Lewisham, London, on Ocotber 24th, 1941, is 5ft 8ins tall, weighs 10st, has brown eyes and curly black hair. Educated at Beckenham Grammar School. Plays a Framus bass guitar and also joins Mick in vocals. Taste in music is R & B. Favourite artists include Jimmy Reed, Chuck Berry, Jerry Lee Lewis, John Lee Hooker and Les Paul from a guitar point of view. Likes astronomy, cashew nuts and books. Dislikes travelling, arriving home at 3 a.m., marmalade and arguments. Clothes: casual, especially leather."

APPENDIX III

Just five weeks after the release of that first No. 1 single, *It's All Over Now*, the Rolling Stones issued on Decca another EP with five tracks, which they called *Five by Five*. A week before it was released, this EP had advance orders totalling 200,000 copies. The group had recorded the tracks at the Chess studios in Chicago, where Chuck Berry, Bo Diddley and Muddy Waters also worked. To coincide with its release, Andrew Loog Oldham issued this press release, with capsuled details – reproduced here in full, like the previous appendix, to show just how The Rolling Stones were being pitched at that time:

FIVE BY FIVE
THE ROLLING STONES

"There is little that has not been said about the commercial impact made by the Rolling Stones over the past year. In this short span of time, they have emerged from relative obscurity into one of the hottest properties in groupdom, surrounded by a fanatical following and a controversial image that is always exploding. Another facet of the Rolling Stones always exploding are their records, and this week sees the release of a new EP from the group, a disc that looks set to beat all their previous records. Already, a week before release, it has an advance order of two hundred thousand. This EP was recorded during the Stones recent trip to America in the studios of Chess Records in Chicago where the discs of Chuck Berry, Bo Diddley and Muddy Waters are made. It is titled *Five By Five* and features five never before released tracks headed off by *If You Need Me*, a Solomon Burke ballad. Two Stones composed numbers complete side one *Empty Heart* and an instrumental picture of Chicago titled *2120 South Michigan Avenue*. The second side features two R & B standards *Confessin' The Blues* and *Round'n Round*.

The Rolling Stones – whose exciting vocal style and unique instrumental sound has set the world alight.

The Rolling Stones – five talented individuals . . . put them together and you have the explosive combination which has captured the Nation's teenagers.

The Rolling Stones – as a way of saying "Thank you" to their friends, their fans, on this EP we have included an additional track.

The Rolling Stones – *Five By Five*

MICK JAGGER
Real name: Michael Philip Jagger
Birthdate: 26–7–44
Birthplace: Dartford, Kent
Height: 5ft 10in
Weight: 10st 6lbs
Colour of eyes: Blue
Colour of hair: Mousy
Parents' names: Joe and Eva Jagger
Brothers and sisters: Brother – Christopher
Present home: Hampstead
Instruments played: Harmonica
Where educated: Dartford Grammar School, London School of Economics
Musical education: None
Age at which entered show business: 18
First public appearance: Marquee Club
Biggest break in career: Meeting rest of Stones
TV debut: Thank Your Lucky Stars
Radio debut: Saturday Club
First important public appearance: Pop Prom, Albert Hall
Disc in bestsellers: It's All Over Now
Disc label: Decca

Personal manager: Eric Easton and Andrew Loog Oldham
Recording manager: Andrew Loog Oldham
Agent: Eric Easton
Biggest influence on career: It varies
Former occupation before show business: Student
Hobbies: Boats, records
Favourite singers, artistes: Chuck Berry, Jimmy Reed, Bo Diddley
Favourite actors, actresses: Sophia Loren, Steve McQueen
Favourite colour: Blue, pink
Favourite food: Continental
Favourite drink: Orange juice
Favourite clothes: Casual
Favourite composers: J. Lieber & Mike Stoller, John and Paul, Chuck Berry
Miscellaneous likes: Driving at night by myself, girls
Miscellaneous dislikes: Motorway cafes, intolerant people

BRIAN JONES
Real names: Brian Jones
Birthdate: 28–2–44
Birthplace: Cheltenham
Height: 5ft 8in
Weight: 10st 1lb
Colour of eyes: Greeny-blue
Colour of hair: Blond
Parents' names: Lewis, Louisa
Brothers and sisters: Barbara (17)
Present home: London
Instruments played: Guitar, harmonica
Where educated: Cheltenham Grammar School
Musical education: Self-taught
Age at which entered show business: 18
First public appearance: Marquee, Oxford Street, W1
Biggest break in career: Meeting other Stones

TV debut: Thank Your Lucky Stars
Radio debut: Saturday Club
First important public appearance: Royal Albert Hall Pop Prom
Disc in best sellers: It's All Over Now
Disc label: Decca
Personal manager: Eric Easton and Andrew Loog Oldham
Recording manager: Andrew Loog Oldham
Agent: Eric Easton
Biggest influence in career: All R & B greats
Former occupation before show business: Various
Hobbies: Women
Favourite singers, artistes: Johnny Cash, Bo Diddley, Jimmy Reed
Favourite actors, actresses: Tony Perkins
Favourite colour: Black/white/grey
Favourite food: steaks
Favourite drink: Milk/whisky
Favourite clothes: "Gear", "Annello" boots, Y-fronts
Favourite band: Muddy Waters band
Favourite composers: Willy Dixon, Bach, Lennon–McCartney
Miscellaneous likes: Having a shower
Miscellaneous dislikes: Public transport
Tastes in music: Very catholic, but I hate brass bands
Origin of stage name: From an old Muddy Waters blues, title seemed apt.

KEITH RICHARD
Real name: Keith Richards
Birthdate: December 18th, 1943
Birthplace: Dartford, Kent
Height: 5ft 10in
Weight: 10st
Colour of eyes: Brown
Colour of hair: Black

Parents' names: Doris and Bert
Brothers and sisters: Nine
Present home: Hampstead
Instruments played: Guitar
Where educated: Dartford Technical School, Sidcup Art School
Musical education: Self-taught
Age at which entered show business: 18
First public appearance: Marquee Club, Oxford Street
Biggest break in career: Meeting the rest of the Stones
TV debut: Thank Your Lucky Stars
Radio debut: Saturday Club
First important public appearance: Pop Prom, Albert Hall
Film debut: Sheik of Araby with Rudolph Valentino
Disc in bestsellers: It's All Over Now
Disc label: Decca
Personal manager: Eric Easton and Andrew Loog Oldham
Recording manager: Andrew Loog Oldham
Agent: Eric Easton
Biggest influence in career: Chuck Berry
Former occupation before show business: Layabout
Hobbies: Sleeping, records
Favourite singers, artistes: Chuck Berry, Shirelles, Crystals, Muddy Waters
Favourite actors and actresses: Paul Newman, Sophia Loren, Jinx
Favourite colour: Black
Favourite food: Chicken
Favourite drink: Orange fruit juice, bloody mary
Favourite clothes: Leather, dark and casual
Favourite bands: Flintstones
Favourite composers: Goffin-King, Chuck Berry.
Miscellaneous likes: Girls, boats, guitars, high heel boots, opium
Miscellaneous dislikes: Policemen, crosseyes, two faced people

Tastes in music: R & B, country music
Origin of stage name: Muddy Waters record *Rolling Stone Blues*

BILL WYMAN
Real name: Bill Wyman
Birthdate: 24.10.41
Birthplace: Lewisham, London
Height: 5ft 8ins
Weight: 10 stone
Colour of eyes: Green-brown
Colour of hair: Black
Parents' names: William, Kathleen
Brothers and sisters: John, Paul, Judy, Anne
Present home: Beckenham, Kent
Instruments played: Bass guitar
Where educated: Beckenham Grammar
Musical education: Piano lessons
Age at which entered show business: 21
First public appearance: Marquee, London
Biggest break in career: Meeting Beatles
TV debut: Thank Your Lucky Stars
Radio debut: Saturday Club
First important public appearance: Albert Hall
Disc in bestsellers: It's All Over Now
Disc label: Decca
Personal manager: Eric Easton and Andrew Loog Oldham
Recording manager: Andrew Loog Oldham
Agent: Eric Easton
Biggest influence in career: Chuck Berry
Former occupation before show business: Engineering
Hobbies: Science fiction, records
Favourite singers, artistes: Chuck Berry, Jimmy Reed, Jerry Lee Lewis, Les Paul
Favourite actors and actresses: Kirk Douglas, Burt Lancaster, Gina Lollobrigida

Favourite colour: Blue
Favourite food: Escalops, scampi, pork chops
Favourite drink: Orange squash
Favourite clothes: Modern, casual
Favourite band: Chuck Berry Combo
Favourite composers: Cole Porter
Miscellaneous likes: Cashew nuts, astronomy, poetry, girls
Miscellaneous dislikes: Arguments, marmalade, travelling
Tastes in music: R & B, popular classics, jazz
Origin of stage name: Who knows

CHARLIE WATTS
Real name: Charles Robert Watts
Birthdate: June 2nd, 1941
Birthplace: London
Height: 5ft 8in
Weight: 10st
Colour of eyes: Blue
Colour of hair: Brown
Parents' names: Mr and Mrs Watts
Brothers and sisters: Linda
Present home: Wembley, Middlesex
Instruments played: Drums
Where educated: Tylers Croft, Harrow Art College
Age at which entered show business: 18
First public appearance: Marquee with Alexis Korner
Biggest break in career: Joining the Rolling Stones
TV debut: Thank Your Lucky Stars
Radio debut: Jazz Club with Alexis Korner
First important public appearance: Pop Prom, Albert Hall
Disc in best sellers: It's All Over Now
Disc label: Decca
Personal manager: Eric Easton and Andrew Loog Oldham
Recording manager: Andrew Loog Oldham
Agent: Eric Easton

Biggest influence in career: Different people in different circles

Former occupation before show business: Graphic designer in London

Hobbies: Women

Favourite singers, artistes: Bo Diddley, Muddy Waters, Mick Jagger, Buddy Greco, Sammy Davis Jr., Picasso

Favourite actors, actresses: All of them

Favourite colour: Red, black

Favourite food: Good

Favourite drink: Tea

Favourite clothes: My taste is too good to answer this one

Favourite band: So many

Favourite composers: George Russell, Gil Evans

Miscellaneous likes: Girls, clothes, myself

Miscellaneous dislikes: None

Tastes in music: Good

Origin of stage name: Ask others

APPENDIX IV

To publicise their first album, the Rolling Stones and their managers Andrew Oldham and Eric Easton issued a press release under the heading "Something To Smile About", illustrated with photos of the Stones boating on the Thames, playing on stage, and relaxing after a session with Gene Pitney. The front-cover photo showed the group smiling; the second page gave details of the album tracks, and then the release continued:

STONE BY STONE
MICK JAGGER
Vocals and harmonica, born Dartford, Kent; age 19. Mick is in his second year at the London School of Economics, but has no idea of economics himself. Likes money and spends it like water. Likes Chinese food, clothes, The Rolling Stones, Bo Diddley, and life in general. Underneath that mousey mop of hair lie two big blue eyes. Has been with the group from its birth.

BRIAN JONES
Vocals/guitar and harmonica; born in Cheltenham, moved to London two years ago. Age 19. Blond-haired Brian smokes 60 cigarettes a day and has packed a lot of different jobs into his 19 years including coal lorry driving; assistant in an architect's office; playing in a jazz band and a year's hitch hiking on the Continent. Fascinated by the railways; wants to be President of the Dr. Beeching Fan Club.

BILL WYMAN
Bass guitar/vocals. Hollow cheeked Bill is 21 and is often called "The Ghost" due to his pale complexion. Interested in

poetry; books; food. Another Chuck Berry fan, Bill has dark hair and hails from Beckenham, Kent.

KEITH RICHARD
Guitar. Black haired Keith was born in Dartford 19 years ago. Has one romance in his life – his guitar! Would like a house-boat on the Thames; collects Chuck Berry and Jimmy Reed records.

CHARLIE WATTS
Drums. 21-year-old Charlie is the "Beau Brummell" of the group. Has over 100 pocket handkerchiefs. "Charlie Boy", as he is called, lives in Wembley, has spent the last year between an advertising agency and The Rolling Stones.

For immediate release on Decca – the long-awaited LP from the Rolling Stones – *Twelve by Five* equals a nutty set of decks from the hippest set of faces to hit beatdom. Face I kicks off with the r'n'b standard *Route 66*. Deck 2 is *I Just Wanna Make Love To You*, but don't take it too seriously, *Honest I Do* features the plaintive vocal and harmonica plea from Mick the Magic Jagger and the fourth set features the compelling *Mona*. Fifth track is an instrumental tribute to two friendly faces that have been closely associated with the boys, Phil Spector and Gene Pitney, entitled *Now I've Got A Witness* (thanks to Uncle Phil and Gene). Side 1 finishes up with *Little by Little*. The lower split of sticks heads off with *King Bee*, *Carol*, *Tell Me*, the Marvin Gaye opus *Can I Get A Witness*, *You Can Make It If You Try* and the Rufus Thomas standard *Walkin' The Dog*.